AF437449

FINDING LIBERTY

Michelle D. King

Permissions:
Scripture taken from the Holy Bible, New International Version®. Copyright © 1973, 1978, 1984 Biblica. Used by permission of Zondervan. All rights reserved.
Scripture quotations marked "NKJV" are taken from the New King James Version. Copyright © 1982 by Thomas Nelson, Inc. Used by permission. All rights reserved. Bible text from the New King James Version® is not to be reproduced in copies or otherwise by any means except as permitted in writing by Thomas Nelson, Inc., Attn: Bible Rights and Permissions, P.O. Box 141000, Nashville, TN 37214-1000.
http://www.nelsonbibles.com/
Taken from the Complete Jewish Bible by David H. Stern. Copyright © 1998. All rights reserved. Used by permission of Messianic Jewish Publishers, 6120 Day Long Lane, Clarksville, MD 21029. www.messianicjewish.net.
ISBN: 979-8-89546-770-1 (sc)
ISBN: 979-8-89546-760-2 (e)

PREFACE

My name is Michelle King. I am a wife, a mother of three boys, and a healing and deliverance minister in Southern Ohio. I own the House of Liberty Healing and Refuge Property, where I conduct and minister healing and deliverance training weekends for people who need personal, hands-on training in spiritual warfare.

I believe in miracles and God's wonder-working power. I have seen mentally ill people clothed in their right minds, nerve damage healed, neuropathy healed, and all sorts of other incredible miracles. God has given me a spirit of childlike faith, awe, and wonder. I believe He is still the same yesterday, today, and forever.

I have been in public ministry since I was a teenager, but I officially started ministering in 2012. In 2012, as an army wife living in El Paso, I started an online support group to pray for soldiers. We warred for them, and it grew to a living room ministry, then flourished to reach thousands. Today, I run an international online healing, deliverance, and spiritual warfare equipping ministry called "Liberty Healing International Church," as well as a school of ministry called "School of Liberty."

My heart is to see the broken restored and the captives set at Liberty, which is why God gave me the name "Liberty Ministries."

This book is dedicated to my husband, Eric King, who fought for me. My parents, the King family, my sisters, my brother and our entire family who were radically affected by this extremely life-changing event in our lives. To my family, thank you for fighting for me and loving me well.

TABLE OF CONTENTS

PART II: Deliverance Prayer Handbook .. 61

CHAPTER
ONE

THE BEGINNING

Jesus came to set the captives at Liberty, and I was that captive.

As I began the journey of writing this book, I felt compelled to highlight my past and dive into the depths of who I was before I found liberty. I attempted to remember all the overwhelming details of my past mistakes, but I confronted an unexpected barrier: writer's block. It dawned on me that I was trying to remove a stone already sealed by the divine closure of the tomb—a tomb where Jesus Christ had laid to rest the burden of my sins. This is the profound beauty of embracing Liberty. In this embrace, our sins are cast into the sea of forgetfulness, vanishing as the distance between the East and the West. They are erased from His divine memory, and if you were to try to remember your sins, they would also be completely erased from your mind. I genuinely believe this is why I struggled to write this story.

When you are giving a testimony, simply telling the story is often enough. Yet, within the details of testimony are certain details that if left out will strip the testimony of its power that can bring deliverance. Jesus made it clear that there was no need for me to revisit the depths of my past. I was not meant to dig up every old sin and dredge up memories of trauma and pain just to offer you a glimpse into my former self. Scripture says, *"and they overcame him by the blood of the Lamb, and by the word of their testimony;"* (Revelation 12:11, KJV). I will share my story as remembered by the blood of the lamb. My purpose in authoring this book is to guide you, the reader, toward the path of Finding Liberty.

My Testimony – The Beginning

I was born crippled with bilateral congenital hip dysplasia, also known as developmental dysplasia of the hip (DDH). It is a condition where the hip joint does not form properly in babies or young children. DDH occurs when the hip joint is dislocated or unstable at birth, and the hip might be misshapen at the top of the femur (upper leg bone) or in the hip socket (part of the pelvis). I experienced miraculous healing from a condition that doctors insisted would require surgery with every significant hip growth. My hip sockets were malformed, and it seemed inevitable that I would undergo multiple hip replacement surgeries, all of which would be funded by the California Crippled Children's Foundation. My prognoses were grim, and the doctors predicted I would not walk until age five, and even then, mobility would be severely restricted. My mom began a quest to prove the doctors wrong. She brought me to many pastors for prayer, and they all spoke of healing to my mom. They would say I would be healed.

My mom, a steadfast prayer warrior, earnestly sought the Lord's healing for me. God revealed to my mother that He would heal my hips and that this healing would strengthen my father's faith in God. My father is a godly man and Christian, but he had witnessed fraud in deliverance healing performed by charlatans when he would take wheelchair-bound people for healing. God revealed to my mom that my healing would increase my father's faith in miracles.

This pivotal moment in all our lives became real after my family gathered while my father laid hands on me, praying for healing. My father held unwavering faith in God's ability to heal, but no one could predict the extraordinary turn of events. My sister said she watched my healing happen before her eyes. She felt so affected that she ran to her bedroom, begging Jesus to come into her heart. She now knew, beyond any doubt, that God is real.

My mother took me to the surgeon for a surgical evaluation, and the doctor's verdict astonished everyone - there was suddenly no need for any procedure. After conducting an ultrasound, the doctor recorded in the medical records that the "procedure worked" despite no surgical intervention from human hands. My parents recognized this as a divine miracle.

Encouraged by this profound experience, they entrusted the x-rays to a respected pastor to share the testimony with the congregation. They were convinced that no tangible proof was necessary to affirm my healing. In a symbolic gesture of faith, they discarded the braces, unaware of the significant impact these decisions would have on my future.

As a little girl, I would profess my healing to everyone.

"I was born crippled," I would tell everyone. I would say this testimony in front of many others.

"God healed me!"

I became keenly aware that I was a miracle child from my earliest years. Yet, as I traversed the tumultuous terrain of childhood, besieged by trauma and the pervasive shadows of this world, my faith became a battleground. Doubt, like a relentless assailant, began to chip away at the bedrock of my belief. How could I be certain of my healing when I lacked tangible evidence? No x-ray, braces, or paperwork - nothing to validate the miraculous transformation I had experienced. In the grip of uncertainty, I became a modern-day doubting Thomas, grappling with skepticism. As doubt wormed its way into my consciousness, my once straight path became twisted and crooked, manifesting in a noticeable gait as I walked through life.

CHAPTER TWO

LOSING MY INNOCENCE

When I was really young, I only wanted someone to spend time with me. I found a friend a bit older than I was who lived nearby, we enjoyed playing games with dolls and painting our nails. Sometimes, if I stayed late enough, we would have ice cream after eating dinner while watching a movie. Sadly, and unknown to me, this little girl was being abused and victimized. She would mimic and standardize the behavior that was being done to her. My friend would hold my eyelids open and force me to watch increasingly sexually graphic movies, starting with movies like American Pie and eventually to more pornographic ones.

Later, she wanted to "play pretend," and this was the time in my life when my childlike, colorful world would be painted gray and black. I was not going to see things the way God had originally intended. After many separate times of "playing pretend," I remember one instance where I had been put in a doghouse, and something very wicked and evil was about to occur. I will spare you the exact details, but the inappropriate behavior suddenly stopped when the little girl heard her name called by her older brother. I remember her being reprimanded for what was going on. The next thing I knew, I had been sent home. As I recall, that was the last time I saw her.

Michelle D. King

Losing my Purity

Around the time I was a pre-teen child, I tried to fit in and be like everybody else. However, I could not ignore the pain and heartache I had experienced. I met new friends who lived across the street from me, but eventually, their parents stopped allowing me to play with them. They claimed that I was too interested in boys, saying I was "boy-crazy." I felt desperate for love and attention, so I sought it out in all the wrong places. I turned to boys, hoping for a sense of worth and safety that I could not find anywhere else.

On my sixteenth birthday, I received an emerald purity ring from my parents, which I felt extremely excited about. We prayed together over the ring. It symbolized my promise to Jesus that I would remain pure. Although I had a few "boyfriends," I intended to maintain a certain standard of purity to save myself for the right guy who would pursue and marry me. I knew he would be my protector and a safe place.

That idea went out the window when I was taken advantage of at a party after I became drunk and high. I lost my virginity in a traumatizing way. I woke up saran-wrapped directly to a bed in the middle of the living room at a high school party. I had no recollection of what all occurred, but I knew it was with more than one boy. I felt a loss of my sense of worth that next morning. The vow I made with the purity ring now seemed worthless because I had betrayed that promise. I believed myself to now be damaged goods. I remember saying to the guy I met at the party, "I am no longer a virgin anymore." He responded, "Well, thanks, I had a good time."

Gradually, I found myself seeking validation in the world around me. Modeling became one avenue to feel loved. The camera lens gave me the affirmation I desperately sought love and affection through. I found my new identity in my physical appearance. However, this pursuit led me down a path of misguided relationships. Desperate for connection, I gave myself to anyone who offered affection or attention. It was a recurring pattern—I craved friendship and sought it relentlessly. One of the photographers ended up being a registered sex offender, and I quickly recognized the evil dark side of modeling.

After realizing that modeling was not my true calling, I turned to performing. I found music gigs on the website Craigslist, and the world became my stage. Within the performing community, I found camaraderie and companionship among fellow artists in my pursuit of belonging. Unfortunately, I soon discovered that they were not always safe to be around.

One such "artist" was also a registered offender. Thankfully, I learned in time that he was not someone I should be associated with. I eventually found a cruise ship entertainment job in Dubai, but my parents did not let me go. Grateful for their refusal, I later knew that it would have put me in a dangerous situation, as human trafficking often occurs in such scenarios.

I went as far as auditioning for a major television show that looked for singers to be the next big 'idol.' I wanted to sing, but I mainly wanted to share what happened to me as a baby with the world. I signed a document stating they could alter my name, background, or anything else to increase their ratings.

I remember making it to the top thirty out of 11,000 contestants. I was in their 'Hollywood round' when they asked me, "Can you tell a joke?" I could not think of any jokes in that moment.

"I'm sorry, but you're just not funny," the guy said. This was how I found out I was not progressing to the next round.

On the way down the elevator, I remember they had cameras in my face, begging me for a response.

"How do you feel about those judges?" they asked, trying to get a rise out of me.

"I am going to go to the beach to enjoy my time, and I am content knowing it wasn't God's plan for me to go to the next round."

As I look back now, I can see the hand of God protecting me all along the way. He was guiding me toward something more than I could understand.

"And we know that all things work together for good to those who love God, to those who are called according to his purpose."
Romans 8:28, NKJV

CHAPTER
THREE

FINDING MY HOPE

Finding My Prince

In January 2012, I attended a local wine tasting, a regular activity for people who grew up in Napa Valley. After returning home, I quickly consumed a bottle of Chardonnay and decided to create an online dating account on Christian Mingle. I sought a Christian boyfriend to attend church with me and pursue a relationship. Before meeting my husband, I prayed for God to bring me a prince who would protect me with his Shield of Armor, see me as worthy, treat me like a princess, and, most importantly, safeguard me. Surprisingly, I found a friend, husband, and protector through God's divine orchestration. Funny enough, my prince was the first and only person I met on the dating site.

After going on dates over a few months, he began truly pursuing me and made it clear that he valued me. When I prayed to God for guidance on whether he was the right person for me, I felt led to search for his name, 'Eric,' online. To my surprise, I discovered that his name meant "Prince." We dated for eight weeks before he left for Army boot camp. During those short eight weeks, we went rock climbing and on hikes; looking back, I realized that these types of dates were all ways for me to trust him and that he would protect me from danger.

While he was away in Army training we wrote letters, love letters. It was in this type of courting, through months of letters back and forth, that we truly fell in love with one another. I started a prayer ministry during this time to support our soldiers while they were away. My very own Army Support Group. On May 25th, Family Day Weekend of boot camp where the soldiers finally get a break and to see their families, I flew to visit him. We took a taxi to the courthouse and eloped in that small town in Georgia.

Eventually, Eric and I had our "official" wedding ceremony on August 5th, 2012. We were married in Napa Valley in a garden pavilion with all our loved ones in attendance. It was straight out of a story book. At the wedding someone gave me the book, *The Power of a Praying Wife*, which became the cornerstone of a ministry I began when the Army stationed us in the middle of the desert sands of El Paso, Texas.

In that year, I started a ministry that I named 'Army Wives Seeking Christ.' The ministry aimed to bring together army wives and teach them how to pray. Despite having little experience in this field, I firmly believed God had called me to serve these women. I learned to teach and minister publicly, faithfully, and diligently in this group weekly.

This is where I began to see the fruit of our prayers; women being healed, marriages healed, and many other miracles. I also learned what it meant to be an authentic leader. We learned to pray for ourselves. We realized that we should not just pray for our husbands, we had to start with ourselves. God had to set us free if we wanted our husbands to be delivered. There are still women from that group in Liberty Healing Ministries to this day.

During that same time in my life, I found myself struggling with my faith. I longed for a faith that could provide solace and comfort, but unfortunately, I felt empty and alone. One day while I walked, I noticed that my gait had become unsteady, and I began to question whether my childhood 'miracle' healing had indeed occurred. These doubts plagued my mind, I longed for inner peace and clarity.

I remember a conversation with a woman who had cancer. Out of my own spirit of unbelief, I asked her, "What if God doesn't heal you? What then? Even Paul had a thorn in his flesh."

My friend and ministry partner then spoke up, telling me I was stealing this woman's hope by asking that question. It soon became clear that my unbelief was beginning to affect me in my own ministry.

That became my own thorn.

Finding Healing

In 2014, I injured my hip, which caused me to seek medical attention. After examining me, the doctor informed me that I had adult recurring hip dysplasia. They recommended that I have a Magnetic Resonance Imaging, or MRI for short, to evaluate the extent of the injury or damage.

Upon hearing the news that I may need hip replacement surgery at the age of twenty-two, I was immediately shocked and saddened. For someone who had always been active and never experienced any significant issues with my hips after my childhood healing, this news took me aback.

I asked the doctor how I could suddenly develop hip dysplasia, given that I had been a track runner, played water polo, and normally walked my entire life without any problems. The doctor explained that hip dysplasia is a common condition that can be present from birth but may not cause any symptoms until later in life. In some cases, the condition can lead to severe joint pain and require surgical intervention, which was my case.

I began my own quest to prove the doctor wrong, not realizing that it was not just for me, but my husband would also be affected. God would use this experience to increase my husband's faith, just as my healing as a child did for my father.

"Eric, what if God reveals that my hips are healed, and I don't need surgery? What if they say I am healed? Would you believe then?" I asked him, feeling optimistic and hopeful.

"Yes, but ultimately, we need to prepare for this surgery. It will affect our lives greatly," he answered, trying to be practical and realistic.

Despite Eric's words, I could not shake off the feeling that I might be healed without undergoing surgery. I kept hearing in my spirit, *"Prepare yourself and arise; take up your bed and walk."* This phrase gave me hope and fueled my belief that I would be healed.

Finally, the day arrived when the MRI results came back. The surgeon called me into the office to speak with me. I felt a mix of excitement and anxiety. Would the results show that I needed surgery, or would they reveal that I was healed, just as I had hoped? I took a deep breath then walked into the doctor's office, ready to face whatever news awaited me.

"Well, there is no need for hip replacement surgery, not only are your hips in the sockets, but there is also an abnormal amount of acetabulum holding them in the sockets, like a sealing of glue that is unexplainable. You tore your labrum, but that should heal right up," the doctor carefully explained. There before my very eyes were the MRI results and the hip X-ray, I had longed for most of my life.

I saw an X-ray image that revealed my hips had an abnormally thick layer of tissue surrounding the joint. I saw a divine imprint, a mark from God signifying that my hips had been touched and healed. The evidence was so compelling that it left no room for doubt. This was a profound moment for me, as it transformed a childhood tale into my personal testimony. Upon returning home, I shared the results with my husband, and together, we prayed and thanked Jesus. Eric had tears of joy in his eyes, this was monumental for him, since he had prayed for the first time about this.

Our lives changed forever.

Finding Hope

"Left tube open, right tube closed," the doctor said during my dye testing at the medical clinic. This testing was after countless other medical tests, many negative pregnancy tests, along with abnormal cycles and consistent letdowns. I asked what it meant, and the doctor explained that my fallopian tube was blocked, which made the chances of conception slim to none. In addition, it would be potentially dangerous for me to get pregnant as I could develop an ectopic pregnancy.

"While you can begin testing and treatments for infertility," the doctor explained, "it is unlikely you would ever conceive naturally."

My husband and I lost hope that we would ever be pregnant. I was barren like Sarah in the bible.

When I realized that I could not conceive despite being healed by God as a baby, I was determined to prove the doctors wrong once again. Before I began seeking out fertility treatment, alongside my Army Wives Seeking Christ group, we prayed fervently for my healing and for other women in the group who had also been diagnosed with infertility.

Despite the group's prayers, my infertility continued to be a problem. I could not understand why God had healed me as a baby but was not allowing me to conceive now. I felt desperate for answers and began seeking other treatments to help me conceive. Before I began any treatments, I received news that my friend had conceived.

This news felt both joyful and painful to me. I felt happy for my friend, but it made me question why God had not granted me the same blessing. I continued to pray for healing and the ability to conceive, but nothing seemed to work. There were reports of several other healings in the group, yet I still faced infertility.

The doctor had also diagnosed me with pre-diabetes, polycystic ovary syndrome (PCOS), infertility, and insulin resistance. By the grace of God, and despite our wavering faith, something miraculous began to happen.

"Well, sign this paper, and we will begin treating you for infertility," the administrator at the clinic said. It was a copy of mumps, measles, and rubella (MMR) vaccine paperwork. The doctors had explained that before they were to start treating me for infertility, I would need to take this shot.

"This immunization will result in a nonviable pregnancy or potential harm to the fetus if taken while pregnant. Please confirm below that you are not pregnant before proceeding," the nurse continued as I reviewed the form.

Since the doctor had diagnosed me with infertility, I signed the paperwork to receive the MMR immunization and begin the treatments. At the time, I felt completely confident that I was not pregnant. However, just a few weeks later, I received the surprising news that I was, in fact, pregnant.

I felt such excitement to share the news with my husband when he returned from his Army training in the field.

"I'm pregnant!" I exclaimed, "You're going to be a daddy!" I did not think of the shot or what the nurse had warned me about it.

Before we knew what was happening, we were facing uncertainty over our pregnancy. We excitedly went to our first appointment to hear the baby's heartbeat, but our hearts were shattered when they told us that they could not find one. We hesitated to trust the military doctors after several appointments because they had changed their prognosis so many times. One moment, they said the baby was dead. Then, they said it could be twins. As we waited for days for a final call, they called to inform me that I might have a tumor and that the baby may be calcifying in my uterus.

When we arrived at the doctor's office to discuss options, we prayed in the waiting room, hoping they were wrong, and that our baby was still alive. At the ultrasound the technician confirmed that there was still a baby. Another military staff member came in, casually drinking coffee while eating a sandwich, and delivered the news that I did not have a tumor, but unfortunately, the baby had not survived. It felt cold and calloused. She suggested proceeding with a dilation and curettage (DNC) procedure. However, my husband was not at peace with this decision, so we made plans to visit a specialist in California.

I flew to California alone while my husband went away on a training mission with the Army. I began experiencing a rapid increase in hormones, which made me appear more pregnant than I should have been. While in Napa, many well-meaning Christian loved ones advised me to "just speak life to your baby." I would go from prayer group to prayer group, with many powerful prayers spoken over me. My mom would pray over my belly and anoint me with oil. I felt extremely ill from the increase in hormones.

We all hoped the baby would be able to survive, but I had a feeling that the baby had not made it. During our final doctor's appointment, the doctor performed an ultrasound and confirmed that the baby had passed away and began to calcify inside me. The doctor explained that my body was not expelling the baby and that I would need to undergo an induction. My mother stayed with me, praying and assisting me through this challenging news.

The doctor gave me 3 options: induce-which means take a pill to induce myself; have a DNC where they could possibly render me infertile and damage my other tube potentially causing an infection; or wait it out and pray that my body discharges it naturally. The last choice would be a potentially fatal decision since it could infect my entire body causing me to become septic. I had been given no suitable options. I waited and prayed over what to do. I knew no matter what that God would be with me. In the end we decided to take the pill to induce labor.

I chose to name my baby Hope. Although it was heartbreaking to lose my baby, the experience also gave me hope that I would become a mother someday. The doctors had been wrong about my ability to conceive, and my womb had been healed. Now, I could cherish the hope in my heart that I would be a mom one day. In September of 2017 I gave birth to my first child, a baby boy.

I found Hope.

CHAPTER
FOUR

FINDING FREEDOM ON MY ROAD TO DAMASCUS

The loss of baby Hope began to take a substantial toll on my faith. *If God could not keep my baby alive, why would He keep me alive?* I thought. This caused the onset of severe symptoms of extreme anxiety. I encountered moments where I tried to calm down by counting my breaths and checking my pulse to ensure I was still alive. I would sit in my bathtub weeping, and begging God to end my life. There were moments I would have visions of drowning myself. The situation started to affect the lives of those around me, especially my husband. Eric would go out drinking with his Army buddies, since that was the military culture at the time, but this only added to the strain we were both experiencing.

"I can't fix her," my husband told our pastor after a considerable fight. "She is constantly at the doctor and thinks everything is wrong with her. I am afraid that one day she is going to have some horrible illness caused by her own hysteria."

"Well, maybe there is some healing that God wants you to do for Michelle. She should see a grief counselor," the pastor suggested.

One day while sitting in my room with tears streaming down my face, I heard the enemy tormenting me in my spirit saying, *"Every single situation you have ever been in, you put yourself in. You are the reason you were hurt as a child; you wanted a friend. You are the reason you lost your virginity at a high school party; you were drunk and high. You are the reason you lost your baby; you took the anti-nausea pills and that vaccine. It's all your fault."*

I called my pastor to tell him these thoughts, seeking counsel from him.

"Michelle, you are not God, you do not give life and you cannot take it away, you are not God," he said to me. "You are not in control and God is the one who opens the womb and closes the womb, it was not His will to bring this baby into the world, there was nothing on earth to stop it, not even you."

I felt set free in my spirit at once. Whatever unclean spirit had begun tormenting me left in that moment. I knew I was not responsible for my miscarriage. God had other plans, He was in control, and He gave me the peace I had longed for over losing my baby. The pastor again encouraged me to seek grief counselor.

I finally followed the pastor's advice to begin seeing a grief counselor once a week and started a book study called "Transformed." My counselor did not just want to discuss the loss of my baby, she also wanted to explore my childhood. She believed there were deeper issues causing my intense anxiety and fear. During these therapy sessions, I started to experience a profound healing in my heart. As part of the process, I found the time to write out heartfelt letters of forgiveness to each person who had caused me pain or wronged me in some way. This therapeutic exercise allowed me to confront and process my emotions. Ultimately leading to a sense of relief and freedom from the burden of resentment and hurt.

During the time I reflected on my struggles, I recognized that these feelings were deeply rooted in the trauma and bitterness I carried from my childhood experiences. I came to understand that my lack of trust in God stemmed from a sense of feeling unprotected during difficult times in my early years. This led to a profound lack of faith in God's ability to bring healing into my life.

I neglected the fact that I had been sexually abused and victimized by a neighbor at a young age. I had concealed all the pain and just moved on, but I had no idea how infected I had become. I had some deep soul wounds that needed to be healed. The very first step to this major spiritual heart surgery was forgiveness. I started forgiving every abuser, every bully, every man who had ever taken advantage of me, and every offender.

Once I released my burdens to God, I began to feel lighter and lighter. This weight being lifted off me had a dramatic effect on my marriage. I no longer weighed down my husband with the burden I had carried into our marriage. This brought healing and hope into our lives, and I finally settled so many hurts in my past. I had no idea that forgiveness would be such a vital part of my deliverance.

Where is my Freedom?

In 2018, I found myself in various leadership roles within my community. I served as a worship leader, a young life leader, and a residential counselor working with abuse victims. Additionally, I served as a leader to a women's ministry. Despite feeling connected to my faith and actively taking part in these important roles, I noticed a shift in my priorities. Instead of fully embracing God's guidance, I found myself prioritizing my desire for friendship and seeking the approval of others again. This started to affect the quality of my Bible studies and evangelism efforts. My ministry to others became influenced by my need to please people rather than staying true to my faith.

When I hung around my non-religious friends, I knew how to consume alcohol in moderation, but due to my low tolerance, it often distorted my judgment. I began to question whether I had fallen into the trap of what some call the "greasy grace gospel," believing that living in grace meant compromising my values. It dawned on me that my understanding of the truth had become skewed. I became skilled at fitting in with different social circles while seeking their approval.

I asked a friend to join one of my Bible studies, hoping to share Jesus' message with her. However, things took an unexpected turn. Instead of discussing spiritual matters, we listened to Eminem, delved into dark topics, and drank together. My original intention to guide her towards faith ended up derailed. I realized I needed to establish credibility before sharing my beliefs that fateful night.

"So, Michelle, I have been meaning to ask you, what do you think about abortion?" she asked.

"You know, who am I to judge?" I said while drinking a glass of wine and opening the fridge for another beer.

"I took one of those plan B pills when I was a teenager, and I took birth control, I used the Nuva ring, so who am I to say whether it's wrong for someone to actually get an abortion. I think if it's early enough, it's different. I may disagree with it, but whatever floats their boat." I spoke aloud.

"Wow!" She exclaimed, "Michelle, you know, you are MY kind of Christian!"

I felt a shiver run down my spine, and a voice within my spirit said, *"You have become the world's kind of Christian. You are an unbeliever's kind of Christian. You are a friend to the world."*

This was how far I had drifted from conviction of truth. I could not stick up for life anymore. It showed how badly I wanted to please the world. I remembered the old, familiar feeling of the spirit of conviction falling upon me.

This conversation put me back on my journey to freedom.

"I'm a believer, God. Your word says I am supposed to have a sound mind. Where is my sound mind? Where is my freedom? Where is my mind of Christ?"

I wrote in my journal these words in big capital letters. I felt angry at God, mad at Him for everything I had been through, even though most of it grew from my own doing. My capitalized letters were not just dramatic; they were filled with rage.

"Where is my freedom, God?"

"Why am I anxious all the time? Why can't I take a vitamin without fearing I am going to choke to death? Why am I afraid my heart is going to stop at any moment? Why am I afraid to go outside? Why do I have visions of shooting myself? Why do I have the desire to drown myself in the bathtub? What is happening to me?"

"What the heck is the point of being a Christian if I don't have freedom?"

My dad had always encouraged me to write in a journal. I wrote these questions repeatedly, emptying my heart to God. It was my primary way of communicating with Him. I wrote letter after letter, pouring out my soul in psalm after psalm. The Lord responded, I wrote down these words from scripture that I felt Him speaking to my spirit:

"The wicked one will no longer pass through you; he will utterly be cut off."

At the time, I had no idea that God was foretelling that He was about to deliver me.

I recall vividly the moment I sat down to write a lengthy letter, pouring out my longing to pray in His Spirit and to find freedom. I was grappling with the concept of having a sound mind and eager to understand its significance. Despite immersing myself in books that dealt with the battleground of the mind, I found myself unable to retain any of the words I would read. My mind was burdened with such an oppressive weight that even when I read scripture, I struggled to grasp and keep its teachings.

To compound matters, I found myself contending with heightened anxiety, which had resurfaced with even greater intensity than before. At the same time, the troubling symptoms of my hip clicking began to reemerge, and I felt consumed by doubt once more. Questions plagued my mind: *What does it truly mean to possess a sound mind? Why do I not experience the mental clarity that scripture promises?*

"Don't go back Michelle"

After journaling about my anger, I searched for a meditative soundtrack. This track claimed to heal any trauma. I wanted it to be Christian, to ensure that I did not engage in anything inappropriate. However, I had no clue what I was opening myself up to. The guided voice started to lead me back to my very first trauma.

Visions of lying on that bunk bed flashed through my mind, forcing me to relive everything that happened to me. The situation felt terrifying, and my heartbeat increased rapidly, beating faster and faster. The experience put me all the way back into a state of trauma. The meditative track sounded so deceitful because while I was listening to the voice, soft music played which gave the illusion of tranquility, but it was anything but peaceful. I once again felt traumatized and found myself in a state of fight-or-flight. If you know anything about mind regression, it can be extremely dangerous.

I felt mentally right back in the memory of being molested as a little girl, with every fear, trauma, and torment returning. Even though I had forgiven my abuser and laid it at the altar before the Lord. I rolled that stone away from the tomb where the feelings were buried and returned to a place I was not supposed to return to. I had opened myself up to extreme demonic torture. I remember feeling strange and reaching out to my childhood pastor. His words stuck with me, "Fill your mind, renew your mind, don't empty it, Michelle. Emptying your mind can put you in danger." This was yet another piece to the life-changing experience I was destined to experience.

My Road to Damascus

The phrase "Road to Damascus" refers to the biblical story of Saul, who converted from Judaism to Christianity while traveling the road to Damascus after he saw a blinding light and heard the voice of God. (Book of Acts, chapter 9) It has long been used figuratively, sometimes put as a "road to Damascus moment."

Weeks later, in September 2018, I received news that my grandmother had passed away from a bladder infection that had turned septic. I flew from Oregon to Idaho, where I met my sister. We stayed up all night, praying and fasting for the healing of my mother's family. We were eager for the entire family to find peace and for everyone to love one another. We specifically prayed that God would help us repair broken relationships. The next day, my sister and I traveled to Los Angeles to attend my grandmother's funeral events and services. My grandmother being Catholic meant that it would be customary to have a rosary and a funeral.

On the day of my grandmother's rosary service, my sister and I stood on the beach saying prayers and fasting more. While we were capturing photos of each other, a magnificent, radiant light suddenly beamed down on us, cascading like a heavenly glow. The light shown down on us like we were being anointed by heaven.

I had no idea that this light would lead to the exposing of all the darkness in my heart and seven days of sleep deprivation - my own road to Damascus.

CHAPTER
FIVE

THE EVENT

The Rosary and The Funeral

Although I have never been Catholic, I grew up with my grandmother bringing me to holiday services at her church. A funeral rosary service in the Catholic Church is a prayer vigil typically held the evening before the funeral Mass. It is a time for family and friends to come together to pray for the repose of the soul of the deceased and to seek comfort in their grief. I kneeled in the pew, praying to Jesus and interceding for my Catholic family members. I started trembling, and my words began mixing and jumbling. I found myself praying in a language I had never heard come from my mouth. This is the moment the Lord baptized me with tongues of fire. I was able to speak in tongues for the first time. When the service ended, I left in the same car as my parents and sister, and we drove away from the church. I realized something incredible had happened to me, which caused me to crave a new perspective.

"I want a new mind. I don't want my mind anymore," I said repeatedly as I hit my head against the car window. My dad began to pray for peace over me, and my mom started to pray for me and my sister. They did not know it then, but they were praying a deliverance prayer for me. I suddenly began to cough, and my hips started burning like crazy. When I got out of the car, I walked perfectly straight. My mom kept repeating, "She's no longer walking like a duck."

Throughout my life, I walked with an awkward gait, almost like a duck, so this felt like a miracle from God. My walk no longer had its crooked rhythm, and my tracks were now straight. That same evening, my sister and I stayed up all night. I felt so amazed by the miracle that had taken place, the new language that seemed to flow effortlessly from my mouth, and shock from my grandmother's passing. There was too much going on in my head. I just could not sleep.

The next day, at the funeral mass, my sister and I were chosen to sing a song during the service. At this point, I had been awake for three or four days and felt very disoriented. I tried drinking water before we sang, but I could not remember if I had already drunk some. I would stare at the glass, lost in thought, just simply trying to remember if I needed to drink water.

After the mass, while walking on the sidewalk, I noticed my feet pointing forward for the first time. I began decreeing and declaring aloud to God, "I believe you healed my hips, God. I repent for not believing I was healed. I command my feet to point forward! You will obey God." "I am healed," I repeated this multiple times, observing as my walk became straighter and my feet were wholly aligned forward. God revealed to me that my lack of faith and belief in my healing had affected my walking. My doubt and uncertainty had caused me to walk crooked and be unstable in all my ways. My family witnessed this miracle, reaffirming that I no longer walked crooked and that my paths had been straightened literally and spiritually.

Faces

While at the Los Angeles airport waiting to catch a flight to Idaho with my sister, and having still not slept in many days, I started seeing cartoon-like images transposed over people's faces. These faces were almost 3D. Words such as "fear" and "sadness" came to my mind with each face I saw. The images on their faces became more pronounced, and I would approach these people to tell them what I saw so I could pray for them. People would look at me like I was strange.

After landing in Idaho, I stayed with my sister. We were both under attack after not sleeping for several days. I felt the need to escape. I tried to drive but physically could not. My dad had to talk me through driving, giving me turn-by-turn directions to a local hotel. By the time I arrived at the hotel I struggled to communicate. I had to ask my dad to speak to the front desk clerk to make a reservation. My dad told me that he felt a sense of calm because he could feel the presence of the spirit of God through the desk clerk, who seemed to understand our situation. I repeatedly asked the clerk if I was safe, and he kindly assured me I would be okay once I got to my room. Even though I did not want to be alone, and for some unexplained reason, this man brought me a feeling of peace. The desk clerk accompanied me in the elevator and all the way to my room. I felt great peace, security, and safety while he escorted me. I believe he was an angel sent to protect me.

I sat alone in hotel room 222, with no way to charge my phone, waiting for my husband to get me. I now had been awake for five days. While on Facetime with my mom, I began seeing strange faces, but this time, I was seeing them clearly in my reflection on my screen. I felt terrified because this new ability felt so unfamiliar to me. I tried explaining to my mom what seemed to be happening. She attempted to tell whatever unclean spirit this was to leave me alone. Suddenly, my face was huge, my mouth opened wide, and I let out a terrifying gut-curdling scream like a strange roar. With no warning, the phone died.

I now knew that whatever was in my reflection was with me. This was the exact moment I decided to take action. I took the Bible from the hotel room drawer and began praying earnestly.

"I am so sick of myself!" I exclaimed in frustration to God. "I don't want to live for me anymore. I don't want to live for this world. I will be your John the Baptist. Please get whatever this thing is out of me, please, God."

I started reading the scriptures on the pages aloud repeatedly. I realize that people probably heard me in the rooms around me, but at this point, I did not care. I just wanted to be free. I knew I had a long time before my husband arrived to get me, and I wanted whatever this was to be gone before he saw me. Many hours passed during this phase of me yelling scripture, getting real before the Lord.

"God, make me your John the Baptist. God, I don't want to be a selfie Christian!" I yelled unashamedly as I prayed aloud.

Scenes of my life played out before my eyes like a convicted reminder of things I had done wrong. Times I had watched inappropriate shows, times I had stumbled other men, times I had hurt people or had been mean to people, times I had hurt other believers. A flashing image after image of every time I had misrepresented Jesus. Each memory brought to my mind led me to remorse and heartfelt cries of repentance. Memory after memory, I poured out my heart before the Lord. I remember the moments I would lay my head against the hotel window, and the sun's rays would shine on my face. It felt as if the very light of heaven was piercing through me.

After hours and hours of this, my husband finally arrived. I could tell by the look on his face that he felt terrified of me. Keep in mind, at this point, I still had not slept for days nor had any food or anything to drink. I was disheveled and needed a shower. My husband saw a woman who appeared homeless and delusional.

Finally, Home

My husband later told me that I would say the most absurd and bizarre things as he drove us down the road. They were strange to him but felt necessary for me to say. During the entire drive home from Idaho to Oregon, I confessed every wrong I had ever done to him and every negative thought I had ever had about him. It was nonstop from the moment we got into the car until we got out. I went as far as to confess things that never occurred or were never said. It felt as if it was not me speaking.

When I exited the car, he saw for the first time that I was walking with a normal stride. I tried to show him my gait had miraculously straightened out, but he did not know what to think because I sounded sleep-deprived and out of my mind.

After entering our home, I saw my one-year-old son but I felt no connection to my child. He was crying and screaming. My very presence frightened him. I climbed up the stairs to our bedroom, and the first thing I laid eyes on was my reflection in the mirror. I saw that awful face still there, covering my face in the reflection. I screamed in utter terror. This frightened my husband so much that he called my mother-in-law to pick up our son. Then, he called our Baptist church pastor to come to our house and pray for me.

I lay on the couch, with my husband next to me, crying at my side, while the pastor prayed and read scripture over me. He asked me to recall the events leading up to sleep deprivation. He wanted to know how it had all led to this point. As I recalled the terrifying events, I felt scared all over again, remembering the faces and the roaring. The pastor then started commanding whatever came to his mind from me.

"Fear, leave her," he would demand.

I would laugh as if something inside of me were taunting him, then sit straight up and suddenly fall back down. "Vanity, leave her!" he commanded at one point. Again, I laughed, sat up straight, and fell back down. This went on for what felt like hours, with him saying different things that came to his mind.

Eventually, since the pastor had not been trained in this type of situation, he told my husband he did not know what to believe if what we were experiencing was just mental or a possession. Essentially, he came to our home believing he was going to pray over and counsel us. During that entire ordeal, I felt as if my brain was being squeezed, and like a thousand filing cabinets were opened all at once in my mind.

When the pastor left, I begged my husband to pray for me. I kept hearing, *"The prayer of a righteous man availeth much."*

"You're a righteous man," I said. "Please, please pray for me."

My husband obediently prayed, and that night, I finally slept. After seven long days of complete sleep deprivation, I finally slept. As I fell asleep, I felt as if my brain was permanently turning off, like I was entering into heaven forever.

"I am going to be a worship leader in heaven. I will finally get to be a worship leader," I told my husband as I drifted into sleep.

I kept thinking there was no way that God would keep me alive after everything I had just encountered and seen. *How would God keep me alive if I knew this much about the spirit realm? How could He keep me alive after seeing all those monstrous faces? There is no way I could learn this much and still live to talk about it.* My thoughts swirled during the first stage of sleep as time seemed to slow down. I remember feeling as if I was slowly passing through a veil.

To my surprise, I awoke the next morning after a whole night of rest. My husband fed me pancakes, and to his surprise, I actually ate them. It was my first authentic meal in days. I remember the dryness of my mouth, the taste of the pancakes, and the dehydration of my throat as they went down.

"Water, water, keep drinking water," my husband lovingly reminded me.

CHAPTER
SIX

YOU HAVE BEEN GIVEN ALL AUTHORITY

In the weeks that followed, my husband returned to work, I needed to deal with my feelings and work through all the changes on my own. Thankfully, my mother-in-law was there for me daily, offering support and a listening ear as I tried to process everything. I was dealing with so many emotions that I decided to take a break from my community responsibilities to focus on resting and caring for myself during this challenging time. Sadly, I was removed from the worship team at the church. I did not understand at the time how harrowing the experience was for the people around me, and to my surprise, the warfare only continued.

The faces were still there.

I found myself constantly surrounded by what looked like cartoon-like faces on everyone around me. To my horror, when I looked in the mirror, those same eerie faces stared back at me. No matter how hard I tried, I could not shake them off. Desperate for help, I sought guidance from a local pastor at a different church, only to be met with disbelief when I mentioned that I, a Christian, could possibly be tormented by a demon. It was then that I realized that these faces were not just figments of my imagination but actual demons. This realization shattered everything I had been taught about spiritual warfare and the belief that a demon could not afflict a devout Christian.

I found myself in a tough spot where I had to face the hard truth that I was dealing with some unclean spirits. Even though I tried talking to my husband about what I was going through, he kept thinking that it was all in my head and that my lack of sleep was the main reason for my mental breakdown. Sometimes, he would take me on long drives, hoping it would help me remember who I was before everything got so complicated.

There is a movie where the main character has dementia and the guy who is interested in dating her takes her on all these dates, but, in her mind, she is experiencing meeting him and going on these dates for the first time. That was what my husband had to do for me. He kept reminding me of how we met, our first date, and all sorts of memories that were hard to recall due to sleep deprivation. He was partly correct; the lack of sleep had a lot of side effects, but it was primarily spiritual warfare.

My husband later said that he felt as if he was losing the woman he loved, the woman to whom he was married. She seemed absent, lost inside her own mind. He would remind me of the beautiful things that defined our relationship - our dates, our letters, our wedding. I struggled to remember them, but I desperately tried to. For months, my mother-in-law had to keep our son out of fear that I would revert to the sleep deprived state I was in when I returned from the funeral. At times, it seemed like I would return to my former self, but whenever I talked on the phone with my sister about the event, I became the scary version of myself all over again. My husband felt very discouraged.

Finding My Authority

I soon had to face the fact that no local pastor, despite their best efforts, could help me. In fact, they told me that my experience was a horror story and that I should not speak of it, or I would just scare people off. I told them this was my testimony and would lead many people to freedom. To free myself from my demons, I went to different events looking for help. Unfortunately, I discovered that some people leading these events were not giving the proper guidance.

In one event, I shared my experience of being sexually abused but later found out that it had been recorded and posted online. The video showed me in a vulnerable state, and they wrongly claimed that I was healed of something I was not struggling with. Seeing these videos online, some with millions of views, made me feel more tormented.

Another event was physically painful from the person leading it, pounding my chest, and forcing my neck back. I would yell that it hurt me, but they kept going, not listening to me, claiming it was the demon coming out. Instead, it was just physically abusive to me. I craved Liberty from these unclean spirits so desperately that I was willing to find it however I could.

During that time, I attempted to confide in my husband, but he still felt overwhelmed with fear and could not accept the spiritual nature of what seemed to be happening. Few people believed me, but my mom, dad, and sister became my most significant support system. They would pray for me, offer counsel over the phone, and try to help me understand it all, even though they were just as puzzled. My husband wanted to shield me from the outside world out of love and concern,. He felt the need to give me time to sort things out and heal.

Instead of taking me to a mental hospital, he sought to protect me from being misunderstood by isolating me.

My revelations about demons and the spirit realm were met with confusion and skepticism in our small town. The rumors spread, and I quickly gained a reputation for being mentally unstable. But I had been awakened and would never spiritually go back to sleep.

One day, I sat in my kitchen and began telling this thing, whatever it was, to leave in Jesus' name. My partner from my old women's ministry in Texas had sent me a book listing different types of demons. I went individually down the list, telling them to leave me in Jesus' name. My stomach would tighten, and my chest would restrict. I kept repeating, "Come out," until I felt a release. I got down on my face in my living room, commanding and repenting for every one of the sins tied to these demons.

The Lord then pointed out the trauma of being molested as a child to me. I knew I was unhealed, and this painful chapter had not been fully dealt with. Although I had written apology notes to my abusers during previous counseling sessions, I never did what I knew in my heart needed to be done. The Lord revealed to me that I needed to call my abuser and tell her that I forgave her face-to-face.

I obediently picked up my cell phone and connected with her on Facetime. I told her that she was forgiven and that I forgave her. I had no idea that this was going to lead to her forgiving the girl who was abusing her at that time. I learned in that Facetime call that she merely acting out what had been done to her. I helped her find forgiveness for her abuse while I forgave her for mine. When I forgave her completely, I felt able to release her and set her free from whatever unclean spirit was within me. However, I realized it was more than one – unforgiveness, bitterness, resentment, and hurt – all demons that entered through that traumatic experience.

The Prayer Tents

Months passed, and I began venturing out into the world again. One day, while driving, I noticed a white tent by the roadside across from a park with a sign that read "Prayer Changes Things." I went up to the tent, but once again, I saw those same demon faces on the people there. I began to pray for the people inside the tent. The leader of the tent invited me to come back and learn about street evangelism. I found a sense of community in that little tent and shared my experiences with the people there. I received support along with ministry from the group, and in turn, I also began ministering to them. Over time, I found relief and support while I learned how to help others. During months of deliverance sessions, I learned how to minister to people and cast off demons myself.

Eventually, I set up a tent at a local park in Prineville, Oregon. My husband had accepted a job as a police officer there after leaving the Army. I put up my own banner that said, "Ticket to Joy, Peace, and Freedom," and "Can we pray for you?" to invite people who needed help. I called this ministry "Freedom Train." I trained a ministry team to join me in helping others. We would hold our meetings in the tent on sunny days and at a local pizza shop on rainy days. We were blessed to see many amazing things happen, like miracles and people finding freedom from their own troubles.

Even though some people did not understand what I was ministering about, I learned to live for God without worrying over what people thought. I remember that my husband would drive by the tent in his patrol car to ensure I was safe. He might not have understood everything that I was doing, but my safety was still his number one priority. He did not share my same beliefs about deliverance or the spirit realm back then, but he supported me fully.

Michelle My Belle

One morning, I sat in my prayer closet, crying to God about feeling abandoned by my friends, saying, "God, I just want to hear you say you love me." I pleaded with Him multiple times to speak audibly to me. I felt so alone and desperately wanted to hear Him sing over and talk to me.

Shortly after that, I stood in a grocery store picking out my favorite ice cream when I heard a song playing through the store speakers loudly. Everything in that moment seemed frozen in time. The lyrics of the song started ringing in my head, "Michelle My Belle, I love you, I love you, I love you."

It was there and then that I knew that God was answering my prayer. It was not the way I expected God to answer my prayer. It obviously was not His audible voice. Yes, it was a Beatles song, and no, I do not particularly agree with them, but it was the words, the timely song lyrics, that I had begged to hear. Finally, I heard Him saying, "Michelle, My Belle, I love you, I love you, I love you, I love you."

I stood in that grocery store, crying as I picked out my favorite ice cream, "Peanut Butter Party," and listened to my heavenly Father sing over me. This was also a song my dad used to sing to me when I was a little girl. I could not help but feel completely loved and adored in that moment.

Later, I was on the phone with someone I was ministering to, and she began to yell, "Michelle My Belle, sing for Him, ring for Him, and awaken His bride. Awaken the Bride!" She was receiving a prophetic word from the Lord. I could feel the Holy Spirit move through me, confirming everything she said. I knew I had heard the voice of God speaking to me that day.

Playing with Fire

My husband surprised me one evening with a spontaneous trip to our favorite pizza place. As we sat in the car, he switched on the radio. A Christian talk show spoke through the speakers, and the host interviewed an author who had written a book titled "Playing with Fire." The author shared compelling real-life stories about spiritual warfare experiences, recounting encounters with supernatural forces. One particularly chilling story involved a woman who was plagued by a voice in her head commanding her to jump out of a window, and she tragically obeyed. Only after receiving deliverance and spiritual help did she realize that the voice was a manifestation of a demon.

She ended up in the hospital, yet immediately after the man ministered deliverance to her, she never heard the voice again. The man shared many other stories similar to hers of individuals he had interviewed. These were people who had stories of being tormented and then being delivered. They were Christians who gave testimony of having demons. The entire time Eric had me listening to this talk show, I kept screaming in my head, *"See!! I am not lying!! This is real!! This was demonic!! I am not crazy!! This was spiritual warfare!"* But I knew in this moment, I had to be still and let God defend me. Which He did.

For the first time, Eric said aloud, "Michelle, I believe you. Everything you said is congruent with what they are saying. I believe you really did have demons and that this sleep deprivation episode really was spiritual. I can see your change, and I know it is real. I know you are not mentally ill." Everything in me celebrated. God defended me. He proved to Eric that what I went through really was spiritual, and I was not mentally ill or crazy. Who knew God would use some political news guy on a Christian talk show to reach my husband? But He did.

This came after two straight years of Eric not believing in deliverance. It was two consecutive years of me begging God to show him that demons were real. For the very first time, my husband believed me. God defended me. All I had to do was be still and let God work in a way that my husband would understand. All I had to do was wait for Him. Those were the longest two years of my life.

CHAPTER
SEVEN

FINDING MY MINISTRY

In kindergarten, I brought a Bible the size of my desk to school. I got in trouble, and my parents were called to come to the school. The principal was concerned about me lugging it back and forth from school. When they asked me why I chose their wedding Bible, which was the size of my desk, I told them I needed a large enough Bible so the entire playground could see the pages. Even as a little girl, God gave me a heart for the masses.

The ministry began during my husband Eric's Army boot camp when he would send me names of fellow soldiers and their prayer needs in love letters. As I interceded for them, I found them on Facebook and added them and their family members to an online prayer group called "Bravo Troop Support Group." In this online group, we prayed for our soldiers and awaited their return from boot camp, discussing their progress and supporting them. I asked everyone to wear white on the day of our soldier's boot camp celebration ceremony. During the ceremony, the commander honored me and the group for our faithful support and prayers. There were waves of people who stood up wearing white shirts.

God gave me a new desire to pray for the Bride of Christ, I began seeing Bravo Troop as representing the Army Bride of Christ. I felt that my Heavenly Father began to cultivate something beautiful in me. One day in Heaven, we will see everyone we have ever touched or poured into wearing white, and our Commander in Chief will say, *"Well done, good and faithful servant."* Bravo Troop always represented the Bride of Christ.

Children's Bread

Eventually, my husband felt he needed to leave law enforcement, so we moved to Idaho temporarily as he went to school. After years of street ministry and deliverance on the side of the road in a tent, I felt led to begin teaching online classes. I named this part of the ministry "Children's Bread," aiming to bring spiritual nourishment to children all over earth. I taught men, women, and children from nations worldwide how to use their God-given authority to cast out demons. I started a deliverance broadcast called "Deliverance is Real" to demonstrate to the world that deliverance is a real and a powerful spiritual practice. On my social media page, I hosted other ministers, shared my own deliverance testimonies, and provided teachings on the subject. Despite facing criticism and being spammed, I felt determined to normalize the practice of deliverance. I taught deliverance before deliverance was popularized. I lost many friends along the way, but I understood this was what it meant to be like "John the Baptist." I had prayed for this, and I received what I prayed for. I persevered through hurt and persecution.

Many people labeled me as crazy and accused me of being mentally ill, but again I persevered. The more I reached out to help others, the more people found relief. Despite facing constant criticism, I continued to help others. I did this tirelessly, sometimes until four in the morning, to help people overcome their challenges. However, this took a toll on my life and relationships, so I had to learn how to find balance and rest. After years of striving for this balance, I finally found a way to offer support online without the added stress on my health or family.

Revisiting the hotel

When my husband attended lineman school in Boise, Idaho, I felt a deep urge to revisit where it all began. The hotel where I had my life-changing experience was just an hour from where we lived. I decided to return to Room 222 in Boise, Idaho.

I asked the desk clerk to let me into the room, explaining that I had experienced a pivotal moment there and felt that God wanted to reveal something more to me about the event. Once I arrived at the room, I requested some time alone. I poured out my heart, thanking Jesus for how far He had brought me since my awakening and for giving me the strength to overcome the naysayers.

I pulled out the same Gideon's Bible from the drawer, it was the exact Bible I had clung to during the sleepless nights, shedding tears and overcoming doubts. I asked the desk clerk if I could keep it, to my delight he said that I could. Then, I shared my story of what happened in that room and prayed with him to receive Jesus. It felt like a triumphant moment, proving that I had overcome the doubts and negativity of the people accusing me of mental illness.

Oil Bottling

"They drove out many demons and anointed many sick people with oil and healed them," Mark 6:13.

My husband was in lineman school, and we were living off our savings.

"God is going to provide for us miraculously," I told him.

Michelle D. King

At the time, I did not know just how miraculous that provision would be. I envisioned filling bottles with oil and sending them worldwide to every Nation. I called this initiative "MyBelle's Blessings." I diligently shipped bottle after bottle to countries across the globe and received many testimonies of people being healed, delivered, and experiencing miracles. I had the amazing opportunity to pray for a woman with AIDS and anoint her with oil. She received miraculous healing.

During that period, my husband and I relied on God's provisions from bottling oil, which, to this day, I continue to ship oil to all nations. I studied the story of the widow who bottled oil with her two sons and shared what I learned with people worldwide, teaching them how to bless and consecrate oil, anoint the sick, and cast-off demons using it. I found where Jesus himself taught to anoint ourselves with oil. *"But when you fast, put oil on your head and wash your face, so that it will not be obvious to others you are fasting, but only to your Father, who is unseen; and your Father, who sees what is done in secret, will reward you,"* Matthew 6:17-18 (NIV). I taught this practice in my ministry as well.

Liberty Healing Ministries

When my husband finished school, we embarked on a new journey, returning to Oregon and settling into my grandfather-in-law's vacant home with our two young sons. During this period, I found myself deeply involved in street ministry. Fueled by this passion, I organized my first conference, "Awaken the Bride." It was a small, yet powerful event held in a local park, where friends from nearby churches joined us to focus on repentance, worship, and deliverance.

This conference was just the beginning of the Liberty Healing Ministries journey. Among our guests were

Spanish-speaking pastors who shared their moving stories, and together, we worked towards inspiring the town to embrace repentance.

In Sunriver, Oregon, I hosted my inaugural healing and deliverance women's retreat training weekend. Women from around the world attended, experiencing freedom, healing, and baptism. This weekend would mark the start of many more deliverance events to come.

My husband and I were eagerly awaiting job opportunities while my husband applied for positions all across the country. After two months of searching, he received an email for a job interview in Ohio. He flew out, was offered the job, and we made the cross-country move from Oregon to Ohio. It was there that Liberty Healing Ministries was officially born.

God spoke to me, saying, *"Set the captives at Liberty,"* prompting me to change the ministry's name. It had evolved from 'Freedom Train' in Oregon to 'Children's Bread' in Idaho, and finally to 'Liberty Healing Ministries' in Ohio. I began hosting healing and deliverance training weekends, which I called "Battle Warrior Weekends," using Airbnb as a venue. Women traveled from all over the United States to experience healing, deliverance, and baptism, much like our earlier events in Sunriver, Oregon. It felt fitting that we landed in Ohio when I discovered that the state motto is "With God, all things are possible."

House of Liberty

During our move to Ohio, we saw sunflowers all along the way. I felt God was confirming His presence, favor, and Divine will to me. During the drive, I commented to my husband, saying, "I will only go where the sunflowers grow and the railroad tracks go."

Eric and I would frequently drive around just to spend time together and share our thoughts. During one particular drive, I shared my dream with him. I wanted to own a property where men, women, and children could come to receive deliverance and healing and then learn how to help others do the same. My husband listened and shared his dream - he wanted a quiet cabin in the woods. I dreamed of having a healing sanctuary where miracles could happen, and he wanted a quiet place in the middle of nowhere.

We began our search for such a place in Ohio, I was pregnant with our third son, and we needed a place quickly since our rental agreement would be ending soon. I posted a photo of us on our local town's Facebook page and received a message from someone interested in selling their home. I initially disliked it when we visited because of the clutter, cigarette smell, and the outside garage had been used as a drinking shack – a man cave so to speak. However, I asked for a sign from God to change my heart if it was meant to be. My husband suggested turning it into a retreat property and building a house on the land since it had twelve acres there was a lot of potential. I still felt hesitant due to the amount of work that would be needed.

One day, on our way to see the house one last time, I asked for a sign from the Lord. A huge rainbow appeared in the sky during a storm, at that moment we passed a sign that said, "Welcome Home Honey." We continued to drive toward the house and passed by several sunflower patches, then we had to cross over railroad tracks. I was reminded of what I said to my husband about only going where sunflowers grow and railroad tracks go. When we drove up the driveway, the house looked different to me, and I started envisioning its potential. I began to see what the house could be and not what it appeared as in the moment. I saw visions of bells, sunflowers, and rainbow - I saw potential and hope.

We decided to make an offer, which was accepted immediately. We worked hard on renovating the house with the help of a minister friend who came from Chicago to paint and assist with the necessary work. We were grateful for his help and transformed the house into a beautiful white canvas. We consecrated the grounds and declared it a place of healing and refuge. This would be another foundation of my ministry, as the house would bring people from all over the world to be saved, healed, and delivered. God was up to something bigger than I had envisioned.

After staking the grounds of our new property, the Lord inspired me to send stakes to different nations. My husband would etch Psalm 91 verses on the stakes, and I would write prayers to help people consecrate their land and properties to the Lord. Many people shared videos of their husbands praying over their land, there were so many amazing stories. I have included the prayers in this book to help you consecrate your land. This began yet another arm of ministry in our Liberty Healing Ministries journey.

Michelle D. King

CHAPTER EIGHT

THE OIL WELL

Every six to eight weeks, our home became a sanctuary where people gathered for healing and deliverance. In the beginning, we had an 800-square-foot garage, that the previous owner littered with beer bottle tops, graffiti-covered wall panels, and still had the lingering smell of cigarettes. It was a mess, with torn walls and an overall feeling of neglect. Yet I heard in my spirit that it would become a place of worship, healing, and deliverance.

I named it the "Oil Well" and took a leap of faith, starting an online fundraiser to transform it. Chair by chair, piece by piece, the Oil Well came to life. It stands now as a conference center on my property where many men, women, and children have experienced healing and deliverance. We witnessed countless miracles and listened to incredible testimonies, backs were miraculously healed, cerebral palsy was healed, marriages became renewed and healed. I have personally witnessed so many miracles that my faith is renewed with each retreat.

During this journey, I stumbled upon another minister's rapid success online. Doubts began to creep in. *Am I doing enough? What am I doing wrong?* My focus shifted from healing and deliverance to gaining followers and achieving greater success. All of which caused me to devalue my accomplishments and feel discouraged by the seemingly small number of people I was reaching. I lost sight of the beauty and blessings around me, clouded by doubt and unbelief. In this valley of doubt, I heard God calling me to rest.

The Bible reminds us in Psalm 23:4, *"Even though I walk through the valley of the shadow of death, I will fear no evil, for you are with me; your rod and your staff, they comfort me."* And in Isaiah 40:31, *"But those who wait on the Lord shall renew their strength; they shall mount up with wings like eagles, they shall run and not be weary, they shall walk and not faint."*

In those moments of doubt and comparison, I learned to lean on God's promises and trust in His timing. The Oil Well stands as a testament to faith, perseverance, and the miracles that unfold when we let go of doubt and embrace God's call to rest and trust in Him.

Leaving the Ninety-Nine for the One

I found myself in a season of rest, and it was clear that God wanted me to take a break from active ministry. One day, while I sat in my garage, a woman running for a local government office walked up my driveway to introduce herself. During our conversation, I mentioned my ministry, and she told me about a nearby church in need of a preacher. Intrigued, we drove to the church property, where I prayed with her, sang the worship song "Yeshua," then made plans to meet the congregation.

Week after week, I preached to this small, traditional church, teaching about healing, deliverance, and putting on the armor of God. Their worship was deeply rooted in hymns, so I made it my mission to learn and play as many hymns as possible on the piano. One hymn, in particular, "It's So Sweet to Trust in Jesus," became a constant comfort to me. Its simple message of trust resonated deeply: "It's so sweet to trust in Jesus, just to take Him at His word, just to rest upon His promise, just to know, 'Thus saith the Lord.'"

We also sang about the blood of Jesus, which I used as a teaching tool to convey the delivering power of His sacrifice. Many were healed and delivered, but only one person at a time, not vast crowds. The church was small, with only five to ten people in attendance. Over time, I felt my assignment there shifting, sensing the need to attract more people to the church. I grew tired and weary, God confirmed to me that my mission there was complete.

I had fulfilled what the Lord sent me to do: to love His people, show them who He is, minister to them, and teach them about deliverance. With this realization, God released me from this assignment, calling me back to my original ministry. He reminded me of the importance of rest and deliverance from busyness.

This experience reinforced the truth of Hebrews 4:10 NIV, which says, *"for anyone who enters God's rest also rests from their works, just as God did from his."* Trusting in God's timing and direction, I returned to my original calling, refreshed and ready to continue the work He had prepared for me.

I returned to the Oil Well.

CHAPTER
nINE

FINDING LIBERTY

In this new season, I began to dance before the Lord and discovered the profound importance of being still while He delivered me. Each time I danced, the Lord brought more profound healing and freedom. In fact, as I write this, I am in the midst of this very season. I am sitting in the Oil Well, anticipating the arrival of eighteen to twenty people in the coming weeks who will come to be saved, healed, delivered, equipped, and trained. I am resting and preparing for the next chapter in this beautiful space.

So, what have I learned from all this? Liberty is about trusting in Jesus, finding peace and rest, and learning to live, walk, and dwell in the Spirit of God. As a deliverance minister, I often get caught up in the numbers, the to-do lists, and the sense of duty. I became robotic, losing the authenticity vital to genuine ministry. But eventually, the Lord reminded me of the importance of authenticity and the value of leaving the ninety-nine for the one.

Little did I know, I was leaving the ninety-nine so God could reach one person: ME! I thought I was stepping away from busyness and the pursuit of numbers to reach just one person in a humble church. But in truth, God was reaching out to me.

He showed me the importance of rest. He showed me that I could be free to be the person He created me to be.

He reminded me of Matthew 11:28-30: *"Come to me, all you who are weary and burdened, and I will give you rest. Take my yoke upon you and learn from me, for I am gentle and humble in heart, and you will find rest for your souls. For my yoke is easy and my burden is light."*

In this season, God showed me that His yoke is easy, and His burden is light. He called me to rest and embrace the simplicity of trusting Him. He left the ninety-nine so He could reach this one. In doing so, God prepared me to better reach others, grounded in His peace and love. God needed to reach this one so I could also reach others who were the one.

I have finally found liberty.

PART II:

Deliverance Prayer Handbook

BELIEVER'S PRAYER

No matter who you are or where you are on your journey, whether you are saved already or seeking to be saved Jesus sees you and knows you intimately. He knows every hair on your head and every mistake you have ever made, yet His love for you remains undeniable. He loved you when you had dark thoughts, when you rebelled, and when you ran away. His love was there when you lied, cheated, robbed, or hurt others. He knows the pain others have caused you, too. His love for you is constant and everlasting.

Right now, Jesus is calling you to choose Him once and for all. The enemy has been deceiving you, making you believe that you lack purpose. But God has bestowed upon you an incredible and powerful purpose to live in joy, peace, and freedom, and to make His name known. The turmoil in the world is a sign of His imminent return.

Today, He is calling you to embrace Him, to accept His perfect forgiveness, and to follow His new plan for your life. Jesus was nailed to a cross and took the punishment we deserved because of His great love for us. Three days later, He arose from the dead, defeating the curse of sin so that we could live in His righteousness. His sacrifice made us brand new, cleansing our sins and making them white as snow. Choose Him today and receive His boundless love and grace. This is the beauty of His forgiveness, mercy, and grace. We never deserved it, but Jesus still loved us. If you are ready to receive His forgiveness and to have your entire life changed pray the following prayer out loud and test Him in who He is.

He will show up and you will experience His Spirit coming upon you in this very moment as you speak.

Michelle D. King

Are you ready?

Do not let the enemy tell you to stop reading. The devil is likely telling you to throw this away. He is probably telling you this is all lies. Do not listen to his voice. Keep reading. Speak your own truth.

1.   Say this prayer aloud so all of heaven hears you.
His word says Anyone who calls upon the name of the Lord will be saved.

> "Jesus Christ of Nazareth, I choose today to make you the Lord of my life.
> I choose today to renounce Satan and every agreement I have ever made with him.
> I repent and I confess all of the messed-up things I have ever done.
> I thank you Jesus that you shed your blood for me, and I receive your perfect forgiveness right now for all of my sin.
> I choose to also forgive those who have hurt me. All of my abusers and release them to you in this moment.
> I believe that you alone are the son of God and the one and only true and living God.
> I give you my heart, my mind, my body, my soul, and my spirit in this very moment.
> Spirit of the Living God, fill me from the crown of my head to the soles of my feet.
> I breathe you in Almighty Breath of God."

2.   Inhale His Breath into Your Lungs
Hold your hands out to Him above. He will fill you and meet you in this moment.

> Continue saying:

"I breathe in your breath of life, your living Spirit God. Fill me with your Spirit. Baptize me and immerse me in your Spirit, Almighty Living God. I choose today to live for you. I choose today to give you all that I am."

3. Your New Identity

When you become born again, all things have become new. The old is gone and the new has come. You are now a child of God. He calls you Holy, Spotless, Righteous, Redeemed and Blameless in His sight. You are brand new. Today, He has called you righteous and your new life starts now.

KINGDOM OF GOD PRAYER

Jesus is now your Deliverer. He is a stronghold of the oppressed and a stronghold for those who are in trouble. Have you been facing torment of any kind in your life? Your mind? God says you can call upon Him and He will deliver you. The enemy seeks to steal your peace, joy, and soundness of mind. But God gave us authority over every fiery dart, lie, or strategy of the devil. It is as easy as telling him to go away and leave you alone. Jesus did it. In the desert, Jesus was under attack by the devil, but He told him to go away.

When you feel tormented or under attack as a new Christian, you can pray to fill your mind, body, and soul with the breath of God, entering into His presence.

1. **State the following:**
    "Jesus Christ of Nazareth, You are God.
    Your word says you were to be called Emmanuel-which means God with us.
    You came in the flesh, were born of a virgin and crucified on the cross for every messed up thought I've ever had, every messed-up thing I have ever done.
    Thank you for your forgiveness, Jesus.
    I choose to also forgive anyone who has hurt me and release them to you now.
    Thank you for rising again and that you are seated at the right hand of the Father.
    Jesus, I give you my heart, mind, body, soul and Spirit, every part of me.
    I ask for your Holy Spirit to fill me from the crown of my head to the soles of my feet.
    Almighty God fill me.
    I breathe you in Almighty Breath of God."

2. Breathe Him In

Take a deep breath in through your nose, and His very Spirit will fill your lungs and breathe His very life into you. Exhale through your mouth.

Scripture References:

"It is the Spirit of God that made me, the breath of Shaddai that gives me life." Iyov (Job) 33:4 CJB

"But it is the spirit in a person, the breath from Shaddai, that gives him understanding..." Iyov (Job) 32:8 CJB

"that as long my life remains in me and God's breath is in my nostrils," Iyov (Job) 27:3 CJB

"Having said this, he BREATHED on them and said to them, "Receive the Ruach HaKodesh!" Yochanan (John) 20:22 CJB

"What I see is that those who plow sin and sow trouble reap just that. At a breath from God, they perish; at a blast from his anger, they are consumed." Iyov (Job) 4:8-9 CJB

These verses are proof that the very breath of God is on your nostrils, the same breath that slays the wicked, breathed into man and gave us life, the same breath Jesus came to give us when he gave up His last breath on the cross so that His BREATH (spirit) could come and live in you!

3. Praise and Thank God

"I thank you for the righteousness of Christ Jesus.
I robe myself in your Righteousness Jesus which is my holy wedding attire in your kingdom.

I take the keys to the Kingdom Gates and enter into
the Kingdom of God of Joy Peace and Righteousness
in Your Holy Spirit right now.
Thank you, Jesus, that I have access to enter into your
kingdom by the blood of the lamb.
I enter into your Spirit, Father.
Father, I look up right now.
Your Kingdom come.
Your will be done in Jesus Mighty name, Amen."

ENTER INTO HIS REST

"Even in plowing time and harvest season you are to rest." - Exo 34

"He answered, "Set your mind at rest — my presence will go with you, after all." Sh'mot (Exo) 33:14

I have learned a lot about the principle of rest. Starting with the very first book of the Bible - Genesis. One of the strongest things God highlighted to me about rest is that on day seven, He rested from all His work so that "it itself could produce." Rest makes the fruit grow. Rest makes the blooms happen. Rest makes the harvest happen. There is no corn without rest. There is no wine without rest, after the grapes are crushed it must be given time to rest. Everyone talks about crushing grapes and oil, but what about rest? There is no oil or wine or even bread without rest. Even dough must rest! Music does not sound good without rest measures. If we do not rest, if the ground does not rest, there is no produce. Rest is vital for the production of fruit.

God-our ultimate example, our very creator, knew the importance of rest. He even called it blessed. Blessed Rest. You can be a good farmer but also forget to rest. I am particularly good at checking things off the list but then listlessness and restlessness can begin to attack. This is often what leads us to feel scatterbrained when we do not rest. God is saying rest so that the work you have done can produce fruit so that it does not go to waste. So that it is fruitful and brings a harvest!

I have learned this from God, yet another one of His character attributes. I have known Him as Healer, Deliverer, Teacher, and Father, and now I am learning He is our rest.

1. Say this Prayer out loud to enter His Rest

"Jesus Christ of Nazareth,
Spirit of the Living God,
I call upon you, and I enter into your rest in Jesus' mighty name.
I enter into your peace, your rest, your calm, your stillness, and your comfort.
I bind and rebuke the spirit of chaos, all the restlessness, mind racing, ruminating thoughts, all the busyness, and command it to leave me now in Jesus' name.
I cast every heavy burden and every yoke unto you, Almighty God.
In Jesus' precious, holy, and mighty name.
Amen"

Scripture References
"Take my yoke upon you and learn from me, because I am gentle and humble in heart, and you will find rest for your souls." Mattityahu (Mat) 11:29 CJB

"My soul, return to your rest! For Adonai has been generous toward you." Tehillim (Psa) 116:7 CJB

*"On the seventh day God was finished with His work which he had made, so He rested on the seventh day from all His work which He had made.
God blessed the seventh day and separated it as holy; because on that day God rested from all his work which He had created, so that it itself could produce. B'resheet (Gen) 2:2-3 CJB*

"For the one who has entered God's rest has also rested from his own works, as God did from his." Messianic Jews (Heb) 4:10

"For this is what Adonai Elohim, the Holy One of Isra'el, says: "Returning and resting is what will save you; calmness and confidence will make you strong — but you want none of this!" Yesha'yahu (Isa) 30:15 CJB

"Therefore, let us do our best to enter that rest; so that no one will fall short because of the same kind of disobedience." Messianic Jews (Heb) 4:11 CJB

"so my heart is glad, my glory rejoices, and my body too rests in safety;" Tehillim (Psa) 16:9 CJB

""Come to me, all of you who are struggling and burdened, and I will give you rest. Take my yoke upon you and learn from me, because I am gentle and humble in heart, and you will find rest for your souls. For my yoke is easy, and my burden is light." Mattityahu (Mat) 11:28-30 CJB

DELIVERANCE PRAYER

No matter what, you have authority over it all. Only do this if you are serious. Do not commit to deliverance if you are not willing to walk it out. This is you making the choice to live your life for Jesus and walk in His joy, peace, and righteousness.

This is deliverance.

1. **State the following:**
    "Jesus, I call upon you now for my deliverance.
    I renounce every spirit of bitterness, resentment, hatred, anger, strife, offense, contention, and I command it to come out of me now in the mighty name of Jesus."

You can say examples of different spiritual areas of bondage:

"Overwhelming Fear, Anxiety, Unbelief, Doubt, Anger, Rage, Frustration, Irritability, Chaos, Confusion, Trauma, Mistreatment, any spirits that came in through abuse, Depression, Dejection, Despondency, Hopelessness, Sadness, Loneliness, every word curse I have ever spoken over myself or anyone has every spoken over me, all doom, gloom, any kind of darkness."

If you have been practicing witchcraft or doing anything to open up any doors to the enemy. Today is the day to close those doors for the last time.

"I receive the spirit of Love, Joy, Peace, Patience, Kindness, Goodness, Faithfulness, Gentleness, Self-Control, Wisdom, Counsel, Might, Revelation, Gratefulness, Contentment, Cheerfulness, Gladness, Thankfulness, Faith into my heart, mind, body, soul, and spirit in the mighty name of Jesus. I breathe in your shalom, your perfect peace."

Keep commanding as you breathe in and breathe out. The Spirit of God, His very breath, will deliver you.

EXAMPLE PRAYER FOR DELIVERANCE FROM DEPRESSION

1. Say the following:
"Lord Jesus, YOU are God, and I give you everything I am. I call upon you right now to heal and deliver me.
Fill me with your joy, God.
Deliver me from this heaviness and depression.
I surrender every part of me to you, Jesus.
My heart, mind, body, soul, and spirit.
I ask for the spirit of the living and true God to fill me, and I call upon you for my deliverance.
Right now.

Thank you, Jesus, for my authority over the enemy and that all demons are subject to me in the mighty name of Jesus According to your written word.

Thank you, Jesus, that according to Psalm 16, at a rebuke and a breath from your nostrils, I am rescued and that your breath slays the wicked, and according to Job, that breath is on my nostrils.

Lord Jesus, I repent, and I confess to you all of my sin. I forgive everyone who has ever trespassed against me. I give them to you God.

(This is a good time to speak who your offenders are.)

And I command every spirit of unforgiveness, bitterness, resentment, hatred, and anger to leave now in the mighty name of Jesus. By the power of the Holy Spirit, and the very breath of God that slays the wicked is upon my lungs. I breathe you in Jesus."

2. Breathe Him In

"Holy Spirit, I breathe you in as I take in this breath!
Thank you for your very breath in my lungs!
Breathe in truth and breathe out the lies.
With each spirit you command, take a big breath.
Remember, spirit means breath.
The power of the Holy Spirit and the very breath of God that slays the wicked is upon my lungs. I breathe you in Jesus. Breathe in truth and breathe out the lies.

Baptize me Jesus with your Spirit, I give you every part of me. Immerse me, God. Overflow in me.

I take authority because you have given me all authority, and I command every spirit of
> Depression
> Heaviness
> Sorrow
> Laziness
> Lack of motivation
> Extreme Fatigue
> Tiredness
> Weakness
> Negativity
> Doom
> Gloom
> Obsessive crying
> Dejection
> Despondency
> (see Spiritual Areas of Bondage list)

To leave me now in Jesus' mighty name as I breathe!"

Just breathe! Let His Spirit (Pneuma-Breath) deliver you!

3. Repent and Forgive

"Lord Jesus, I repent, confess to you all of my sin, and I forgive everyone who has ever trespassed against me. I give them to you, God.

(This is a good time to speak who your offenders are.)

And I command every spirit of unforgiveness, bitterness, resentment, hatred, and anger to leave now in the mighty name of Jesus. By the power of the Holy Spirit, and the very breath of God that slays the wicked is upon my lungs. I breathe you in Jesus."

4. Loose the Fruits of the Spirits

Say the following:
"I loose the spirit of love, joy, peace, patience, kindness, goodness, faithfulness, gentleness, and self-control into my heart, mind, body, and soul in Jesus mighty name.
I receive your joy, Jesus.
Holy Spirit, Fill me from the crown of my head to the souls of my feet with your Spirit and your oil of joy."

End this by getting on your face before the King of Kings and the Lord of Lords, praising Him as He fills you!

Spiritual Areas of Bondage

Here is a list of potential spiritual areas of bondage. Remember to ask God to search and know you. Let God reveal what He wants to deliver you from.

ABANDONMENT-
Strongman

Isolation
Loneliness
Not feeling wanted
Not belonging
Victim
Rejection

ADDICTION-Strongman

Physical Addictions
Alcohol
Caffeine
Nicotine
Opiates
Cocaine
Uppers/Stimulants
Marijuana
Any other street drug
prescription drugs

Mental Addictions
Sex
Pornography
Masturbation
Gambling
Video Games
Television
Sports
Exercise
Other People
Receiving Attention
Adrenalin

ANGER – Strongman

Frustration
Wrath
Hatred
Rage
Resentment
Temper
Bitterness
Tantrums
Spoiled Behavior
Feeling Bad Inside
Hidden Anger (Associated
w/High Blood Pressure)

ANXIETY- Strongman

Burden
False Responsibility
Fatigue
Heaviness
Nervousness
Restlessness
Weariness

BITTERNESS- Strongman

Blaming
Complaining
Critical Judging
Gossiping
Murmuring
Ridicule
Unforgiveness
Irrational Condemnation

COMPETITION –
Strongman

Competitive when Driving
Jealousy Feelings
Possessiveness Feelings
Striving to out-do everyone
Pride
Competing when
unnecessary
Competing with everyone
and everything

CONFUSION-Strongman

Confused Thoughts
Indecision
Lack of Focus
Lack of Concentration
ADD Label by doctor
ADHD Label by doctor
OCD Label by doctor
Disconnected Thoughts
Lapses in Memory
Inability to make
conclusions
Distorted Perception
Hear Words That are not
Said
Take things in an overly
sensitive manner
Unable to grasp simple
truths

DECEPTION – Strongman

Confusion
Lying- Self & Others
Self-deception
Gullible
Believing Lies

DEPRESSION –
Strongman

Feeling of Discouragement
Feeling of Despair
Feeling of Hopelessness
Despondent
Self-pity
Over-Sleeping
Insomnia
Thoughts of Suicide
Attempts of Suicide
Withdrawing from Others
Feeling Alone…No One
Understands
Feeling like a Victim

ESCAPE – Strongman

Fantasizing
Lethargic Feeling
Passivity
Procrastination
Withdrawal from Others
Forgetfulness

FEAR – Strongman

Fear of other people
Fear of going outside
Fear of Sex
Fear of Eating
Fear of Talking
Fear of Driving
Fear of Exercise
Fear of Bathing
Fear of Anything That is
Important to Daily Survival
Fear of Men
Fear of Women
Fear of Relationships
Fear of Commitment
Fear of Success
Fear of God
Fear of Jesus
Fear of Churches

Fear of Government
Fear of Rules
Fear of Rejection
Over Sensitive Nature
Fear of Illness (Infirmities)
Fear of Cancer
Fear of Diabetes
Fear of the Dark
Fear of High Blood Pressure
Fear of Heart Attack
Worry About Everything
Projected Fears & Worry
Doomsday Fears
Heavy Anxieties
Burdens
Heaviness
Horror Movies
Superstitions
Irrational Concerns
Numerous Phobias
Fear of what you might say

FINANCIAL PATTERNS
– Strongman

Greed
Stinginess
Spend too Much
Compulsive Shopping
Poor Financial Judgment
Inability to Save
Inability to Budget
Live in Poverty
Job Losses
Poor Employment History
Move Job to Job
Fail at your Jobs

GREED – Strongman

Cheating
Covetousness
Idolatry

Stealing
Misrepresentation
Fraud
Do Anything for Money
Unable to Spend Money

GRIEF – Strongman

Feeling of Loss
Feeling of Sadness
Feeling of Sorrow
Feeling of Suffering

INFIRMITIES/SICKNESS /DISEASE – Strongman

Illness through Accidents
(Fall, Cars, Injury, etc.)
Arthritis
Asthma
Bareness
Cancer
Diabetes
Family History Disease
Fatigue
Fibromyalgia
Heart Disease
Hypertension
Miscarriage
Mental Illness
Migraines
Skin Diseases/Rashes
Premature Death
Physical Abnormalities
Sexually Transmitted
Disease
High Blood Pressure
Vision Problems

MENTAL ILLNESS – Strongman

Feeling of Craziness

Compulsions
Confusion
Hallucinations
Hysteria
Insanity
Obsessive Compulsive
Schizophrenia
Paranoid
Seizures- All Types
Mental Anguish
Shock Treatments
Lobotomy

**OCCULT /
WITCHCRAFT** –
Strongman

Astrology
Black Magic
White Magic
Wicken
Clairvoyant
Mind-Reading
Palm-Reading
Spirit Box
Ghost Box
EVP
Instrumental Trans-
communication
Talking to the Dead
Crystal Ball
Divination
ESP
Calling or Dispatching
Demons
Fortune Telling
Tarot Cards
Automatic Handwriting
Free-Masonry
Eastern Star
Horoscopes
Telepathic
Teleportation

Pendulum
Psychic Healing
New Age Medicine
Past Life Readings
Non-Christian Exorcism
Necromancy
Occult Jewelry or Clothing
Ouija Board
Taken or Made a Blood Pact
or Oath
Levitation
Hypnosis
Watched "The Exorcist"
Movie and Became VERY
Frightened
Read Occult and/or
Witchcraft Books
Watched a Horror Movie
and Became VERY
Frightened
Attended a Séance
Talked to spirit guides
Read Books about Spirit
Guides or New Age?
Sorcery
Practiced Yoga (which is
worship of the Earth/Sun
goddess)
Practiced Eastern Medicine
or Martial Arts
Voodoo
Visited a so-called
"Spiritist?"
Visited Pagan Temples

REBELLION – Strongman

Stubbornness
Undermining
Lying
Insubordination
Argumentative
Hard-Headedness

Michelle D. King

Argue to be Arguing
Debating

REJECTION – Strongman

Perceived Rejection
Perfectionism
Self-Rejection

RELIGION

Anti-Christ
Cults
Legalistic Thinking

SEXUAL SINS –
Strongman

Fornication
Exposed Yourself
Homosexuality
Incestual Sex
Lesbianism
Fantasies of Lust
Lustful Masturbation
Demonic Being Sexually
Assaulted You
Pornography
Premarital Sex
Rape
Seduction
Sexual Abuse
Prostitution or Sex for
Money
Sex with an Animal
Frigidity With Spouse

SHAME – Strongman

Condemnation
Embarrassment
Guilt
Self-accusation

Self-Disgust
Self-Reproach

PRIDE – Strongman

Arrogance
Self-Importance
Vanity
False Self-worth
Feeling Better Than Others
Plastic Surgery for Vanity
Reasons
Criticizing One's Own
Appearance
Disliking One's Own Race
Disliking One's Own
Nationality
Criticizing Your Appearance

STRIFE – Strongman

Arguing
Bickering
Cursing
Dissension
Disagreement
Discord
Mocking
Blaming
Friction

SURGERIES – Strongman

Anesthesia
Difficult Childbirth
Epidurals

TRAUMA – Strongman

Been in a Car Accident
Other Types of Accidents
Suffered Major Loss
Suffered Sexual Abuse

Suffered Date Rape
Suffered Physical Abuse
Suffered Verbal Abuse
Suffered Violence
Suffered Emotional Abuse
Any Major Traumatic Event

UNBELIEF – Strongman

Doubt
Disbelief
Rationalism
Skepticism
Unbelief
Doubt Everything
Do not Trust Anyone
Cannot Believe Anything
Everything Seems Dubious

UNWORTHINESS –
Strongman

Feelings of Inferiority
Self-hate
Self-condemnation
Self-mutilation
Self-torture
Feeling Undeserving
Feeling of Unworthy
Feel Second Rate

VIOLENCE – Strongman

Feuding
Arguments
Physical Harm
Murder
Retaliation – I am going to
get you!
Torture
Threats

DELIVERANCE FROM IDOLATRY

If you are ready to burn your idols. After saying the general prayer, read this prayer aloud in a posture of humility. A beautiful way to posture yourself before your King is to get on your knees.

1. **Say the following:**
   "Jesus Christ, you are God.
   You are my deliverer, my healer, and my Savior.
   I give you my heart, mind, body, and soul.
   I believe you came in the flesh, died on the cross, and rose again. You are seated at the right hand on the Father, and you are Adonai.

   Thank you for your blood that was shed for me Jesus.
   I repent, God, and confess all my sin to you.
   Please send your Holy Spirit to fill me from the crown of my head to the soles of my feet.

   Thank you, Holy Spirit, that your very breath is upon my lungs, the same breath that slays the wicked. I give my breath to you, Jesus.

   Thank you, Jesus, that I have been given all authority to trample over serpents, scorpions, and over all the power over the enemy and that nothing by any means shall harm me. Thank you, Jesus, that all demons are subject to me in your name and your power. God, I forgive all my abusers and give everyone who has ever hurt me to you, Jesus.

   Right now, I take authority, and I confess as sin every spirit of IDOLATRY, SELF IDOLATRY, IDOLIZING MAN."

This would be a good time to ask God what your idols are. An idol would be anything that takes up your thought life more than Him. We pay homage with our thoughts as worship.

"Father, I repent of all idolatry.
I repent of burning incense to false gods.
-addiction and idolatry of Facebook
-addiction and idolatry of social media
-addiction and idolatry of my phone
-addiction and idolatry of my computer.
I repent of using my body to worship other gods unknowingly.
I repent of not worshiping you in Holy attire.
I repent of not glorifying you with what I wear.
I repent of all idolatry in my life, God.
Reveal all things to me, Almighty Spirit of Truth.
I burn up every false idol on my altar before you now with the fire of the Almighty Consuming God.
Almighty God, refine me.
Burn within me and burn up all desires and gods I have worshiped or idolized in any way.
Search me and know me. Deliver me, God.
Father, I renounce the false gods of bitterness, resentment, hatred and anger, fear, and sin to you and break agreement with it.
I take authority of it and command it to leave me now in Jesus' name."

2. Breathe Him In

This is a good time to ask the Holy Spirit what else?
Is there fear? Rejection? Self-rejection? Ask Him to search your heart and know you, and command everything He reveals to leave.

Remember to Confess, break agreement, and renounce each one!

3. Loose the Fruits of the Spirits

Say the following:

"I loose the spirit of love, joy, peace, patience, kindness, goodness, faithfulness, gentleness, and self-control into my heart, mind, body, and soul in Jesus mighty name.

I receive your joy, Jesus.

Holy Spirit, Fill me from the crown of my head to the souls of my feet with your Spirit and your oil of joy."

DELIVERANCE FROM IMPARTATION

A prayer for deliverance from demonic impartation and transfer of demonic spirits. There has never been a more important time to search your heart and see what demonic teachers have been teaching you and false prophets, and false teachers are very real.

1. **Say the following:**
    "Father, I confess as sin all idolatry and making demonic covenants, and I break all demonic covenants and contracts with all demonic leaders known and unknown. I break all demonic soul ties, mentally, emotionally, physically, or spiritually, with ___________________ and command every demonic impartation or transference of spirits to leave me now in Jesus' name.

I command every spirit of idolatry, idolatry of man, spiritual harlotry, vain glory, vanity, vain pursuits, people pleasing, fear of man, deception, dishonesty, greed, greed for gain, kundalini, any Hindu god of Hiram Abiff, freemasonry, any demon that came in through laying on of hands, all confusion, deception, mind binding spirits, mammon, manipulation, error, false Jesus, false fire, false Holy Spirit, false anointing, false impartations, false teaching, false doctrine, false religion, all demonic doctrines to be removed from my heart, mind, body soul and spirit now in the name of Jesus.

I burn out all demonic seeds with the fire of God and call crop failure on all demonic fruit that has come from demonic teachings or doctrines of demons…

I come out of agreement with all false prophecies and false prophetic words that have been spoken over my life, and I command every demonic word to be broken now in Jesus' name.

I break all word curses, and I come out of agreement with every demonic witchcraft curse that has been placed on me and command every hex vex spell or incantation to be broken now in Jesus' name.

I sever all silver cords, and I remove my name from every demonic Altar now in the name of Jesus Christ of Nazareth, who came in the flesh.

Every demon that has come upon me through Spiritual, harlotry or spiritual covenants, made financially mentally emotionally or spiritually I break now in the mighty name of Jesus, by His blood and by His power.

Father, I receive your spirit of truth, Almighty God, I receive your spirit of clarity, wisdom, revelation, and counsel.
I put on my helmet of salvation, my breastplate of righteousness, my belt of truth, and my shoes of peace in Jesus' name.
Father, I receive the gift of discernment in Jesus' name, Amen.

2. Breathe Him In

This is a good time to ask the Holy Spirit what else? Ask Him to search your heart and know you and command everything He reveals to leave.
Remember to Confess, break agreement, and renounce each one!

3. Loose the Fruits of the Spirits
Say the following:
"I loose the spirit of love, joy, peace, patience, kindness, goodness, faithfulness, gentleness, and self-control into my heart, mind, body, and soul in Jesus mighty name.
I receive your joy, Jesus.
Holy Spirit, Fill me from the crown of my head to the souls of my feet with your Spirit and your oil of joy."

DELIVERANCE FROM THE SPIRIT OF ERROR

If you have been yoked to a false teacher, false ministry, false prophet, false anointing, or any falsehood whatsoever, I have written a prayer for your deliverance from any demonic impartation, agreement and to cancel all yokes below.

What is the spirit of error?

The spirit of error is what causes the twisting of scripture and false teachings to be formed. This is the exact opposite of the spirit of truth! God calls us to live and walk in the spirit of truth, but when we wrongfully divide the word of God, we walk, preach, and teach in a spirit of error. The spirit of error is what Christians invite when they begin walking in falsehood and teaching false doctrine. This is a spirit that ministries and teachers easily fall prey to if they are not disciplined in their understanding or studying of scripture. The spirit of error takes our eyes off the truth and the mission of furthering the gospel and instead causes us to be spiritually invested in falsehood and false spiritual practices that cause us to divert from hearing God clearly.

This spirit will lead to an undiscerning heart, thus darkening our understanding and leading to futility of mind and foolishness. Be careful you do not develop an undiscerning heart. It also is the prime reason many become vulnerable and susceptible to the schemes and tricks of false teachers and false prophets.

Guard your mind.

When you give up your mind, you give up your ability to discern properly. Jesus gave you a mind for a reason.

Guard it at all costs. Your heart, too. Do not become spiritually lazy. Do not forsake testing the spirits. Testing the spirits is not about whether someone is loving or kind. We are called to test for a spirit of error.

Truth seekers, you have the Spirit of Truth in you who reveals all things. Let Him teach you discernment and test the spirits. Remember that Satan comes as an angel of light, and the Antichrist will bring "false peace" and deceive many including the elect.

Scripture References
"For false christs and false prophets will rise and show signs and wonders to deceive, if possible, even the elect." Mark 13:22

'They are of the world. Therefore, they speak as of the world, and the world hears them. We are of God. He who knows God hears us; he who is not of God does not hear us. By this we know the Spirit of truth and the spirit of error.' – 1 John 4:5-6.

"because, although they know who God is, they do not glorify him as God or thank him. On the contrary, they have become futile in their thinking; and their undiscerning hearts have become darkened. Claiming to be wise, they have become fools!" Romans (Rom) 1:21-22

"But you, dear friends, since you know this in advance, guard yourselves; so that you will not be led away by the errors of the wicked and fall from your own secure position." 2 Kefa (2 Pe) 3:17

DEMONIC IMPARTATION FROM THE SPIRIT OF ERROR AND SPIRITUAL LAZINESS DELIVERANCE PRAYER

There has never been a more important time to search your heart and see what demonic teachers have been teaching you. False prophets and false teachers are very real. Call upon the right Jesus, not this false Jesus that people are preaching these days. You will need to renounce the false Jesus below. Remember, He could very well say He never knew you. This is not a joke.

1. **Say the following:**
    "Jesus Christ of Nazareth,
    You are the one and only true and living God.
    I believe you came in the flesh,
    died on the cross, rose again on the third day, and are seated at the right hand of the Father.
    Jesus, I choose to serve you, and only you and I give you every part of me.
    My heart, my mind, my body, my soul, and my spirit.
    Fill me with your Holy Spirit today, Almighty God.
    Father, I repent, and I confess as sin all idolatry and making demonic covenants, and I break all demonic covenants and contracts with all demonic leaders known and unknown.
    I repent of giving into a spirit of error and believe I am spiritually lazy.
    God, I repent of ever unknowingly teaching the spirit of error.
    I repent of ever yoking to the spirit of error.
    I repent of not testing the spirits and yoking myself to false teaching.
    I repent of chasing after man's anointing.

I break all demonic soul ties, mentally, emotionally, physically, financially, or spiritually with ________________and command every demonic impartation or demonic transference of spirits that came in through ________________ to leave me now in Jesus' name.

I command every spirit of idolatry, idolatry of man, spiritual harlotry, vain glory, vanity, vain pursuits, people pleasing, fear of man, deception, dishonesty, greed, greed for gain, confusion, mind binding spirits, mammon, manipulation, error, false Jesus, false fire, false Holy Spirit, false anointing, false impartations, false teaching, false doctrine, false religion, all demonic doctrines to be removed from my heart, mind, body soul and spirit now in the name of Jesus. I burn out all demonic seeds that have been planted in my mind, soul, or spirit and uproot all demonic teachings. I burn them up with the fire of God and call crop failure on all demonic fruit that has come from demonic teachings or doctrines of demons…

I come out of agreement with all false prophecies and false prophetic words that have been spoken over my life, and I command every demonic word to be broken now in Jesus' name.
I break all word curses, and I come out of agreement with every demonic witchcraft curse that has been placed on me and command every hex vex spell or incantation to be broken now in Jesus' name.
I sever all silver cords, and I remove my name from every demonic Altar now in the name of Jesus Christ of Nazareth, who came in the flesh.
Every demon that has come upon me through Spiritual, harlotry or spiritual covenants, made financially mentally emotionally or spiritually I break

now in the mighty name of Jesus, by His blood and by His power.

Father,
I receive your spirit of truth, Almighty God,
I receive your spirit of clarity, wisdom, revelation, and counsel.
Father, I receive the gift of discernment in Jesus' name, Amen."

2. Breathe Him In
This is a good time to ask the Holy Spirit what else?
Is there fear? Rejection? Self-rejection? Ask Him to search your heart, know you, and command everything He reveals to leave. Remember to Confess, break agreement, and renounce each one!

3. Loose the Fruits of the Spirits
Say the following:
"I loose the spirit of love, joy, peace, patience, kindness, goodness, faithfulness, gentleness, and self-control into my heart, mind, body, and soul in Jesus mighty name.
I receive your joy, Jesus.
Holy Spirit, Fill me from the crown of my head to the souls of my feet with your Spirit and your oil of joy."

IMPARTATION OF THE FRUIT OF THE SPIRIT

Many of you may know about demonic impartation, but do you know as a child of God who walks in the spirit of God, you can also impart the spirit of love, joy, and peace into others? When we speak, we speak blessing and life. We can bind demons, but we can also loose or impart blessing.

The seven spirits of God are the Spirit of the Lord and the Spirits of wisdom, understanding, counsel, might, knowledge, and fear of the Lord. They are associated with Jesus, who holds them along with seven stars. The seven spirits first appear in Revelation 1:4 and are before the throne of God.

"For I long to see you, that I may impart to you some spiritual gift, so that you may be established, that is, that I may be encouraged together with you by the mutual faith both of you and me." Romans 1: 11-12, NKJV

Remember, we can bind demons, but we can also loose the SPIRITS of God! By saying I loose the spirit of ___(ex. Love)___ into my *(or who you are ministering to)* heart, mind, body, soul, and spirit in Jesus' name. This is how we speak life!

1. Say the following:
"Father, fill me with the spirit of _________*(insert one from the list below.)*

I loose the spirit of _____________into my heart, my mind, my body, my soul, and my spirit in Jesus' name."

GODLY FRUITS OF SPIRIT

These are the names of Godly fruit in scripture that we can impart to others and also be filled with ourselves.

Fear of the Lord
"And he will be filled with the spirit of the fear of the Lord. He will not judge according to the sight of the eyes, nor reprove according to the hearing of the ears."
Isaiah 11:3

Grace
"And I will pour out upon the house of David and upon the inhabitants of Jerusalem, the spirit of grace and of prayers. And they will look upon me, whom they have pierced, and they will mourn for him as one mourns for an only son, and they will feel sorrow over him, as one would be sorrowful at the death of a firstborn."
Zachariah 12:10

Life
"When they were standing, these stood

still. And when they were lifted up, these were lifted up. For the spirit of life was in them." *Ezekiel 10:17*

Meekness
"What would you prefer? Should I return to you with a rod, or with charity and a spirit of meekness?"1 Corinthians 4:21

Precious
"Whoever moderates his words is learned and prudent. And a man of learning has a precious spirit." *Proverbs 17:27*

Prudence
"And you shall speak to all the wise of heart, whom I have filled with the spirit of prudence, so that they may make the vestments of Aaron, in which, having been sanctified, he may

minister to me."
Exodus 28:3

Spirit of Goodness
Spirit of Revelation
Spirit of Counsel
Spirit of Might
"But the fruit of the Spirit is love, joy, peace, longsuffering, kindness, goodness, faithfulness, gentleness, self-control. Against such there is no law." Galatians 5:22

Spirit of Wisdom
"so that the God of our Lord Jesus Christ, the Father of glory, may give a spirit of wisdom and of revelation to you, in knowledge of him." Ephesians 1:17

Truth
"But when the Advocate has arrived, whom I will send to you from the Father, the Spirit of truth who proceeds from the Father, he will offer testimony about me." John 15:26

GENERAL PRAYERS

With any prayer you intend to use in this section of the book, you will always start with this simple general prayer.

1. First state your declaration of faith:
"Jesus Christ of Nazareth, I believe you are the one and only true and living God.
I believe you came in the flesh, you were born of a virgin, crucified on the cross, rose again the third day, and that you are seated at the right hand of the Father.
Thank you, Jesus, for your blood that was shed for me and for your perfect forgiveness that you gave your life to give me.
Father, I confess all sin known and unknown.
I give you my heart, my mind, my body, my soul, and my spirit.
Spirit of the living God, fill me from the crown of my head to the soles of my feet.
I breathe you in Almighty breath of God."

2. Breathe Him in.
Take a deep breath in through your nose, and His very Spirit will fill your lungs and breathe His very life into you. Exhale through your mouth. Practice this anytime you see "**Breathe Him In**" throughout this entire section of the book.

3. Repent and Forgive
"Lord Jesus, I repent, confess to you all of my sin, and I forgive everyone who has ever trespassed against me. I give them to you, God."

(This is a good time to say who your offenders are.)

"I command every spirit of unforgiveness, bitterness, resentment, hatred, and anger to leave now in the mighty name of Jesus. By the power of the Holy Spirit, and the very breath of God that slays the wicked is upon my lungs. I breathe you in Jesus."

4. **Next Break Soul Ties by saying:**
"I break all demonic soul ties mentally, emotionally, physically, electronically, financially, spiritually, and sexually with __*Say name of individual*___, and I command every unclean spirit that imparted or transferred to come out of me now in the name of Jesus Christ of Nazareth."

Daily Arming Prayer

"I put on my full armor.
My Helmet of salvation and deliverance
My breastplate of righteousness
My belt of truth
My shoes of peace
My sword of the spirit
My shield of faith
And I put on love, tender mercy, and compassion in Jesus' mighty name."

Ephesians 6:10-18, NIV - The Armor of God

[10] Finally, be strong in the Lord and in his mighty power. [11] Put on the full armor of God, so that you can take your stand against the devil's schemes. [12] For our struggle is not against flesh and blood, but against the rulers, against the authorities, against the powers of this dark world and against the spiritual forces of evil in the heavenly realms. [13] Therefore put on the full armor of God, so that when the day of evil comes, you may be able to stand your ground, and after you have done everything, to stand. [14] Stand firm then, with the belt of truth buckled around your waist, with the breastplate of righteousness in place, [15] and with your feet fitted with the readiness that comes from the gospel of peace. [16] In addition to all this, take up the shield of faith, with which you can extinguish all the flaming arrows of the evil one. [17] Take the helmet of salvation and the sword of the Spirit, which is the word of God. [18] And pray in the Spirit on all occasions with all kinds of prayers and requests. With this in mind, be alert and always keep on praying for all the Lord's people.

Michelle D. King

Blessing Oil

Here is a general prayer for blessing oil.

How to bless oil
Take your oil, put your fingers in it, and say the following:

"Father, I bless this oil in the name of Jesus Christ by the power of the Holy Spirit and the shed blood of Jesus Christ. I consecrate it for your Glory and for your Kingdom. I loose healing, joy, peace, and deliverance in Jesus' name. Father, use this oil to set the captives free and to heal the sick.
Begin to pray in the spirit.
I bless this oil, Jesus.
May it be like Paul's handkerchief or the liquid hem of your garment in Jesus' mighty name, Amen."

If you have a prayer language, use it. Pray over your oil intently.

Consecration

Scripture says for us to offer ourselves as a living sacrifice set apart for God. For this pleases Him. Romans 12:1 The second part of the verse is, "By the renewing of our mind." How do you renew your mind? By filling it with truth. The word of God is used to renew our minds and wash them.

His living word will renew, revive, and cleanse your mind daily. Then, there is one more step - walk in obedience. If you have set yourself apart, now it is time to hold up our end of the deal. Which means now we are to live and walk in holiness and not do the former things we used to do before we were set apart.

A Quick Prayer for Consecration
Every morning, when you wake up, give yourself back to God.

Say: "God, I give you my heart, my mind, my body, my soul, my spirit, my emotions. I set them apart for you, Jesus."

This is the easiest way to consciously set ourselves apart.

Morning Consecration Prayer
Bless your head with oil
Bless your eyes with oil
Bless your mouth with oil
Bless your hands with oil
Place your hand over your heart, and bless that also.

"Father, I consecrate my heart, my mind, my body, my soul, my spirit, my eyes, my mouth, my emotions, my hands, every part of me to you, Almighty God, in Jesus' mighty name by the power of the Holy Spirit.
I command all exhaustion, fatigue, tiredness,
(Anything you need to take authority over)
to leave me now in Jesus' name.

Jesus, I give you every part of me.
I ask that you use me for your glory.
I loose the spirit of love, joy, peace, patience, kindness, goodness, self-control, wisdom, counsel, might, understanding, comfort, grace, mercy, and clarity into my heart, mind, body, and soul in Jesus' name.
I breathe you in Almighty breath of God.
(Breathe)
Thank you, Jesus, for being the very breath upon my lungs.
I consecrate my lungs to you in Jesus' name.
May every part of me be an instrument of worship unto you, Adonai!
I enter into your spirit, Almighty God.
I choose to live and walk in your spirit, not my flesh or emotions.
I enter into your kingdom of joy, peace, and righteousness in the Holy Spirit right now, in Jesus' name.
Thank you, Jesus. Amen."

Esther Soaking Prayer

Soaking Prayer while being delivered, sanctified, and cleansed spiritually and physically while in a bath.

1.   Anoint Your Bathing Space.
Cleanse and anoint the walls while saying,
> "I consecrate this to you, Jesus, for your glory and your kingdom, and I bless this bath now in Jesus' name."

2.   Anoint Yourself.
Say this out loud while anointing your head with oil, pouring water on your head, and washing your body.
> "Jesus Christ who came in the flesh was born of a virgin, died on the cross and rose again for my sin, who is God and is seated at the right hand of the Father, I believe in you and confess you as my Savior, My Healer, Deliverer, and my God. Holy Spirit, fill me from the crown of my head to the soles of my feet.
> Immerse me, Holy Spirit.
> Baptize me in fire.
> Baptize me in your spirit, God."

(This is a good time to dunk your head)

3.   Ask Him to Baptize You in His Living Water.
Say this before you go under the water,
> "I give you every part of me, my heart, mind, body, soul, and spirit.
> Everything I am, is yours, Jesus.
> Baptize me in your living water."

Dunk your head, let Him baptize you. This is an incredibly beautiful experience. Soak with Him. Breathe Him in. His fragrance is sweet, and His aroma is pleasing.

4. **Ask for Forgiveness.**
"Father, I repent and confess all my wrongdoings to you, and I receive the forgiveness you died on that cross for, and I thank you for your blood that covers all my sin.
Thank you, Jesus, for forgiving me.
I choose to forgive everyone who has ever hurt me, and I release them to you in Jesus' name.
I forgive ___________________."

5. **Claim Your Authority.**
"Thank you, Jesus, that you have given me all authority to trample over serpents and scorpions and over all the power over the enemy and that nothing by any means shall harm me. (Luke 10:19)
The anointing and the authority are in You. Ask God to search you, know you, and see if there is any wickedness in you and less you into His ways of everlasting."
Remember, cast means to evict. We are taught to cast our cares and anxieties.

6. **Take Authority.**
"Right now, I take authority over every spirit that is not of you.
Every spirit of _______________________________
(Examples: bitterness, resentment, hatred, anger, unforgiveness, trauma, abuse, word curses, sickness, infirmity, anger, fear, anxiety, deception, confusion, religious, legalism. See list of Spirits.)

Leave me now in the mighty name of Jesus, by the power of the Holy Spirit, and the shed blood of Jesus Christ."

7. Breathe Him In.

Spirit means breath. It leaves by breath. Powers of the air. Breath. The word says that the breath of God slays the wicked. That breath is in you.

Say, "Thank you, Jesus, for your breath that slays the wicked, and I breathe you in. I breathe out any spirit that is not of you now in Jesus' name."

With each spirit you command, breathe.
Inhale and exhale.
Rinse, Wash, Repeat. Let Him cleanse you.

Begin to ask Him, "Search me and know me, Jesus, if there is anything I need cleansing from. I consecrate my entire life to you. Deliver me, Almighty God."

He will be faithful, and He will show you. Enjoy your time with your Healer, Deliverer and Purifier.

I Can Do All Things Prayer

The Bible says in Philippians 4:13, "I can do all things through Christ who strengthens me." When God says "all," He means it. The devil, known as the father of lies, creates strongholds through the lies you have believed about yourself. A powerful way to break free from these lies is to apply the Word of God and dismantle these strongholds.

Start by making a list of everything you have limited yourself in—every area where you have believed you could not succeed. Contrast this with what Jesus says you can do. Identify the lies Satan has told you and replace them with the truth of Christ's promises. This exercise will help you realize that through Christ's strength, you are capable of overcoming any obstacle and achieving all that God has planned for you.

1.   **Say this aloud:**
     "Jesus, I can do all things through Christ who gives me strength including__________________ (name whatever you have been limiting yourself in. *Example (tell my testimony out loud, speak in front of groups, be a good listener, whatever it is)*
     And I command every lie that comes against that to leave me now in the mighty name of Jesus."

Then say it again.

     "I can do ALL things."

2.   **Breathe in His truth. Breathe out the Lies.**

Prayer to Look Up

Change the way you wake up. Look up. It is time we learn to live in the Spirit. When we react in our flesh or live in our flesh, we produce death and destruction. When God says to look up, He is telling us to enter into the Spirit.

This is the same language David used when he said he could not look up because of his troubled heart (Psalm 40:12). It is the same expression used when Stephen, filled with the Holy Spirit, looked up to heaven as he was being stoned to death (Acts 7:55-56). It is precisely what Jesus meant when He told us to "look up" during perilous times when darkness covers the earth (Luke 21:28).

We, as spirit-filled Christians, need to master the ability to live in, walk in and abide in the spirit. To live in the Spirit is life, but to live and walk in the flesh is death. Our spirit hears God because He is Spirit. We operate from heavenly realms, and this is the spirit realm, the realm of the Spirit, not our flesh.

The natural man cannot understand the mysteries of the Spirit realm; only the spirit man can comprehend them. To look up is to live in the Spirit, to seat yourself in your rightful heavenly realm and see through the eyes of the Spirit, hear through the ears of the Spirit, and abide in the Spirit.

1. **Pray this aloud.**
    "Adonai, Elohim,
    I call upon you to fill me with your spirit Almighty God.
    I choose to look up.
    I choose to live in your Spirit.
    I enter into your Spirit, Almighty God.
    I call my spirit forward now in Jesus' name to receive and understand the things of your Spirit.

I choose to let my spirit be led by your Spirit and to put off the desires to be emotionally or carnally led.
Spirit of the living God, fill me from the crown of my head to the soles of my feet.
Immerse me with your Spirit.
Baptize me once again, every day.
I choose to abide in your Spirit, and I crucify my flesh today, every day, starting today.
In Jesus mighty name, Amen."

<u>Scripture References</u>
"What I am saying is this: run your lives by the Spirit. Then you will not do what your old nature wants."
Galatians (Gal) 5:16

"For who knows the inner workings of a person except the person's own spirit inside him?
So too no one knows the inner workings of God except God's Spirit.
Now we have not received the spirit of the world but the Spirit of God, so that we might understand the things God has so freely given us.
These are the things we are talking about when we avoid the manner of speaking that human wisdom would dictate and instead use a manner of speaking taught by the Spirit, by which we explain things of the Spirit to people who have the Spirit.
Now the natural man does not receive the things from the Spirit of God — to him they are nonsense!
Moreover, he is unable to grasp them because they are evaluated through the Spirit.
But the person who has the Spirit can evaluate everything, while no one is in a position to evaluate him.
For who has known the mind of Adonai?
Who will counsel him?

But we have the mind of the Messiah!" 1 Corinthians (1 Co) 2:11-16

"Use all the armor and weaponry that God provides, so that you will be able to stand against the deceptive tactics of the Adversary. For we are not struggling against human beings, but against the rulers, authorities and cosmic powers governing this darkness, against the spiritual forces of evil in the heavenly realm. So, take up every piece of war equipment God provides; so that when the evil day comes, you will be able to resist; and when the battle is won, you will still be standing. Therefore, stand! Have the belt of truth buckled around your waist, put on righteousness for a breastplate, Always carry the shield of trust, with which you will be able to extinguish all the flaming arrows of the Evil One. And take the helmet of deliverance; along with the sword given by the Spirit, that is, the Word of God; as you pray at all times, with all kinds of prayers and requests, in the Spirit, vigilantly and persistently, for all God's people." Ephesians (Eph) 6:11-14, 16-18

"But the fruit of the Spirit is love, joy, peace, patience, kindness, goodness, faithfulness, humility, self-control. Nothing in the Torah stands against such things." Galatians (Gal) 5:22-23

"Therefore, as God's chosen people, holy and dearly loved, clothe yourselves with feelings of compassion and with kindness, humility, gentleness and patience." Colossians (Col) 3:12

"Remember, I have given you authority; so you can trample down snakes and scorpions, indeed, all the Enemy's forces; and you will remain completely unharmed." Luke (Luk) 10:19

Prayer to Open Your Spiritual Eyes

"In the name of Jesus Christ of Nazareth, I take authority over every demonic spirit, all spirits that are blocking my spiritual vision, all spiritual blindness, spiritual deafness, spiritual lameness, spiritual apathy, whatever is causing a lack in my vision, all spiritual veils, cloudiness, mind fog, natural and spiritual come out of my eyes now in the name of Jesus.

Spirit of the Living God, I call upon you to open my spiritual eyes. Just like Elijah prayed for his servant to see, I ask that you open my spiritual eyes so that I may see clearly in your spirit, Almighty God.

I command my spiritual eyes to be opened in the spirit right now in Jesus' name.

Thank you, Jesus, for opening my spiritual eyes.

I receive sight in the Spirit in Jesus' name."

Prayer to Open Your Spiritual Ears

"In the name of Jesus Christ of Nazareth, I take authority over every demonic spirit. I bind and rebuke every deaf and dumb spirit and command you to come out of me now in Jesus Mighty name."

Sound Mind Prayer

Your mind is incredibly important, and Satan seeks to destroy it and create chaos within it. Guard your heart and your mind. Avoid cursing your own mind with negative words. Stop saying things like "I feel crazy," "I'm losing my mind," or "I am so scatterbrained." Avoid cursing others' minds by saying things like "she's crazy." Remember, Jesus says we will eat the fruit of our lips (Proverbs 18:21). Your own words can testify against you.

Instead, speak the truth of Scripture over your mind. You have been given power, love, and a sound mind (2 Timothy 1:7). This is your weapon, and it is exactly what the devil wants to steal from you by lying and telling you that your mind is not sound. If your mind feels bound, it is unsound. So, unbind it with the truth of God's Word and live in the promise of a sound mind (Philippians 4:7).

1. **Say this aloud:**

    "I have a sound mind and the mind of Christ, and I command every lie that comes against that to leave me now in Jesus' name. I bind my mind to the mind of Christ."

2. **Breathe Him In.**

Treasures Forevermore Prayer

You can access endless treasures at any time as a Kingdom resident living in Liberty. Those treasures are called "fruits." Fruits of Righteousness. Fruits of the Spirit. In fact, only those who walk in the Spirit can have access to these fruits. They are yours but only if you choose to be filled with His Spirit that produces these treasures and this fruit. This is what we feast on as born-again, Spirit-filled, Spirit-led children of God feast on. Fruit.

Do you want Love? Do you want Joy? Do you want patience? Do you want to be more kind? Do you want goodness? Do you want to be more faithful? What about humility? Do you want more self-control? Want wisdom? Jesus says, Get wisdom. Want insight? Get insight.

All you have to do is access the Kingdom, the Spirit of God, where that treasure is located. But it does not stop there. Every good and perfect gift is from above. There is a treasure, good fruit, and any good gift available to you as a Kingdom resident walking in liberty.

1.   Say the following aloud:
Raise your hands up in the air in a receiving position and be filled!

"Jesus Christ of Nazareth,
I thank you for your sacrifice.
I thank you for your forgiveness and that I am robed in your righteousness.
I thank you that you have given me access to the fruit of your Spirit and of righteousness and that I can feast on that fruit every single day as you fill me increasingly in abundance.
Father, I thank you that you have given me the keys to the Kingdom.

I take the keys to the Kingdom, and I enter into your Kingdom, God.
I enter into your Spirit, Almighty God.
(Remember this is something you can pray daily out loud.)
Father, I receive the spirit of love.
I receive the spirit of joy.
I receive the spirit of peace.
I receive the spirit of wisdom, counsel might, understanding, revelation…
In abundance.
Fill me, Lord.
I receive these fruits from your Spirit into mine, Jesus.
Into my heart, my mind, my body, my soul, and my spirit.
In the mighty name of Jesus.
By the blood and the power of Yeshua, the Messiah.
Amen."

<u>*Scripture References*</u>
"And this is my prayer: that your love may more and more overflow in fullness of knowledge and depth of discernment, so that you will be able to determine what is best and thus be pure and without blame for the Day of the Messiah, filled with the fruit of righteousness that comes through Yeshua the Messiah — to the glory and praise of God." Philippians (Php) 1:9-11 CJB

"But the fruit of the Spirit is love, joy, peace, patience, kindness, goodness, faithfulness, humility, self-control. Nothing in the Torah stands against such things." Galatians (Gal) 5:22-23

"What I am saying is this: run your lives by the Spirit. Then you will not do what your old nature wants." Galatians (Gal) 5:16

Michelle D. King

"For this very reason, try your hardest to furnish your faith with goodness, goodness with knowledge, knowledge with self-control, self-control with perseverance, perseverance with godliness, godliness with brotherly affection, and brotherly affection with love.
For if you have these qualities in abundance, they keep you from being barren and unfruitful in the knowledge of our Lord Yeshua the Messiah. Indeed, whoever lacks them is blind, so shortsighted that he forgets that his past sins have been washed away." 2 Kefa (2 Pe) 1:5-9

"The beginning of wisdom is: get wisdom! And along with all your getting, get insight!" Mishlei (Pro) 4:7 CJB

"This is how my Father is glorified — in your bearing much fruit; this is how you will prove to be my follower."
Yochanan (Jhn) 15:8

"For the old nature wants what is contrary to the Spirit, and the Spirit wants what is contrary to the old nature. These oppose each other, so that you find yourselves unable to carry out your good intentions." Galatians (Gal) 5:17 CJB

"But the wisdom from above is, first of all, pure, then peaceful, kind, open to reason, full of mercy and good fruits, without partiality and without hypocrisy. And peacemakers who sow seed in peace raise a harvest of righteousness." Ya'akov (Jas) 3:17-18

SPECIFIC PRAYERS FOR AFFLICTIONS

Abandonment

Father, I thank you that you have never abandoned me or forsaken me and that I am accepted fully into your beloved. I bind, and I rebuke every unclean spirit of abandonment, forsaken, grieved in spirit, loneliness, cast away, cast aside, neglect, outcast, every spirit that came in through feeling unwanted, and I command you to come out of my heart, my mind, my body, my soul and my spirit in Jesus Mighty name.

Abortion

Father, I thank you that your bloodshed was shed for my bloodshed. I repent, Lord, of the lives I have taken into my own hands and for the sin of murder. I confess all sin to you, Jesus, and I give this baby to you, Lord. I thank you that by your grace and your mercy that one day I will get to meet my baby in heaven. Father, I choose to release myself of all shame, condemnation, and guilt I have held onto for my sin, and I receive you perfect forgiveness Jesus; thank you for your grace, your mercy and your blood that was shed on that cross to cover this sin of murder. God, I repent.

I confess all sin of abortion, every sacrifice that was done to Moloch, every spirit of death, spirits that came in through hatred of children. I bind and rebuke you, unclean spirits, and command you to come out of my heart, my mind, my body, my soul, and my spirit now in Jesus' name. I command all affliction, infirmity, sickness, bareness to come out my ovaries, come out of my inward parts now in Jesus' name. Father, I receive you spirit of life abundance, of joy, of laughter, of newness and grace into my heart, my mind, my body, my soul, and my spirit in Jesus' name. I prophesy life to my womb, life to my uterus, life to my ovaries. I prophesy restoration and healing to my inward parts in Jesus' name. Thank you, Jesus, for new life.

Abuse

Father, you know what it means to be abused, mistreated, and hated. God, you know my pain, and you know the hurt I have carried from the trauma of this abuse that has been in me for years. God, I choose to forgive my abusers and release them to you, every offender, and everyone who has ever hurt me. I choose to cast every sin they have ever done into the sea of forgetfulness and remember no longer. I bind, and I rebuke every demonic spirit that came in through abuse, mistreatment, torment, and criticism. Perversion, hurt, sexual abuse, mental abuse, physical abuse, rape, molestation, all cults, all religious leaders, all trauma, and I command you to come out of my heart, my mind, my body, my soul, and my spirit in Jesus mighty name.

Anger

Lord, your word says that Love is patient and Kind and is not easily angered. I repent, Lord, that I have been easily angered and not been very patient. I confess as sin my anger, my impatience, my rage, my quick temper. I bind and rebuke every demonic spirit of rage, anger, fury, gall, hatred, bitterness, resentment, anger, impatience, agitation, frustration, animosity, spite, outrage, hostility, violence, murder, retaliation, revenge, foolishness, all anger to come out of my heart, my mind, my body, my soul and my spirit in the name of Jesus Christ of Nazareth.

Anguish

I thank you, Jesus, that you are my comforter and my healer, and I confess that my heart and my mind has been vexed. Lord, I break agreement with the spirit of anguish, distress, agony, pain, torment, misery, grief, sorrow, torture, heartache, all sadness, and command you to come out of my heart, my mind, my body, my soul, and my spirit in Jesus might name.

Depression

Father, I thank you that your word says to put on a garment of praise for my heaviness. I put on that garment right now in your spirit, Almighty God, and I take authority, I bind, and I rebuke you every demonic spirit of heaviness, depression, dejection, despondency, hopelessness, sadness, melancholy, and command you to come out of my heart, my mind, my body, my soul and my spirit in Jesus' name.

Fear

You have not given me a spirit of fear but of love, power and a sound mind, and I command every lie that comes against that to be torn down now in Jesus' name. Father, I receive that sound mind in Jesus' name. I confess all sin of fear, of not trusting in you, of worry, of anxiety, of paranoia. I break agreement with every spirit of fear, anxiety, worry, paranoia, madness, suspicion, distrust, apprehensiveness, all heavy burdens, albatross, false burdens, false responsibilities, false cares, and all foreboding and dread, and I command it to come out of my heart, my mind, my body, my soul and my spirit in the mighty name of Jesus Christ of Nazareth. I cast all my anxieties, my cares, and my burdens unto you, Almighty God.

Feeling Crazy

Father, you have promised me a sound mind and so I claim my sound mind in Jesus' name. I have the mind of Christ, and I command every lie that comes against that to leave me now in Jesus' name. I bind, and I rebuke every spirit of insanity, madness, neurosis, hysteria ,delirium, disorientation, mania, psychosis, derangement, paranoia, mental illness, craziness, all mind binding and mind racing spirits, restlessness, listlessness, chaos, lunacy, every spirit attacking my mind - I command you to come out of my mind, my heart, my body, my soul and my spirit now in the name of Jesus Christ of Nazareth.

Night Terrors

Father, I thank you that your word says, I need not fear the terror of the night, so I take authority and I bind and rebuke you spirit of terror of the night, all horror, all terror, all fear, all night terrors, all sexual demons, all fear of nightmares, all fear of the darkness, all fear of sleeping alone, all fear of the night, anxiety, social anxiety, separation anxiety, every demonic spirit that came in through the eye gates, all demons that came in through the ear gates or in through the mind come out now, all fear that came in through horror movies, all fear come out now in the name of Jesus Christ of Nazareth. It helps to anoint the head of the child if it is a child needing ministry in this area. I loose the spirit of peace, comfort, rest, and perfect shalom into the heart, mind, body, soul, and spirit in Jesus' name.

Pride

Father, I humble myself in your sight right now. I repent, and I confess the sin of pride to you, Jesus. I confess all sin of rebellion, vanity, self-exaltation, self-promotion, self-worship, and self-centeredness to you, and I break agreement with those spirits now in Jesus' name. I bind and rebuke every spirit of pride, rebellion, vanity, self-exaltation, self-promotion, and all self-idolatry and self-centeredness, and I command you to come out of my heart, my mind, my body, my soul, and my spirit in Jesus Mighty name.

Religiosity and Unbelief

I thank you, Lord, for the fact that you have given me a new spirit and new wine. Lord, I do not want to be a religious-minded person anymore. I choose instead to be led by your spirit. Even if that makes me look foolish. You use foolish things to confound the wise. I confess as sin all of my religious mentality. I bind and rebuke every demonic spirit of unbelief, doubt, religiosity, legalism, dogma, all traditionalism, all spirits that came in through being close-minded and not allowing you to lead me, Jesus. I command every demonic spirit of religiosity to leave me now in Jesus' name. I loose the spirit of childlike faith, awe, wonder, belief, and hope into my heart, my mind, my body, my soul, and my spirit in Jesus' name. I believe in You, Lord, help my unbelief.

Sexual Immorality + Pornography

I confess as sin, and I break agreement with, and I repent, Lord, of all sexual immorality. I bind and rebuke every demonic spirit that came in through pornography, erotica, books, movies, YouTube, Netflix, sexual sin, homosexuality, lust, uncleanness, lesbianism, immorality, lust of the eyes, lust of the flesh, adultery, incest, rape, masturbation, prostitution, shame, guilt, condemnation, defilement, all lust of my eyes, every demonic spirit I have allowed to come into the gates of my eyes. God, your word says that I will set no unwholesome thing before my eyes, and I have allowed my eyes to see darkness and allowed filth to come into my eye gates. Your word also says, how great that darkness will be if I let it in. I choose Father to break agreement with this darkness. I consecrate my heart, my mind, my body, my soul, my spirit, and my eyes to you, Almighty God.

I anoint my eyes with you eye salve from Heaven with fresh oil and sanctify, cleanse, and wash my eyes by your spirit, your water, and your blood in Jesus' mighty name, Amen.

Sickness

I bind and rebuke every demonic spirit of infirmity, sickness, malady, disorder, say the name of the disorder, cancer, arthritis, inflammation, blood disease, bone disease, chronic sicknesses, ailment, infection, affliction and disease and command you to come out of my heart, my mind, my body, my soul, and my spirit in Jesus' name. Come out of ____ *say the region of the body*____.

(This could be the throat, the neck, wherever the infirmity or the affliction is located. This is where you would command the spirit of infirmity to come out of. Be specific.)

Sleep Deprivation

Father, your word says you give your beloved rest, and I claim that promise over me now in Jesus' name. I bind, and I rebuke every demonic spirit of insomnia, sleep deprivation, restlessness, mind racing, mind binding, driving, pressure, busyness, all demons attacking in the midnight hour. I command you to come out of my heart, my mind, my body, my soul, and my spirit in Jesus' name. I loose the spirit of rest and perfect peace into my heart, my mind, my body, my soul, and my spirit in the name of Jesus.

Spiritual Wisdom and Understanding

Father, I thank you that you said to ask for spiritual wisdom and understanding. So, I choose today to get spiritual wisdom and understanding. I put up my hands to you, Almighty God, and I receive the spirit of wisdom, I receive the spirit of understanding, I receive the spirit of revelation, I receive the spirit of counsel in Jesus' name.

Trauma

In the name of Jesus, I bind and rebuke every unclean spirit that came in through trauma, and I command you to come out of my frontal lobe, my amygdala, come out of my brain, the neurons of my brain, come out of my nerves of my brain, come out my muscles, my joints, come out of the memory recall now.

SPIRITS

Here is a list of different spirits and oppressed states of spirits mentioned in the Bible. Jesus gave us all authority over the enemy. These are spirits that were created by God but used by the enemy to oppress us. We have authority over them.

Spirit of Anguish

"And so, Moses explained all these things to the sons of Israel, who did not agree with him, because of their anguish of spirit and very difficult work."
Exodus 6:9

Spirit of the Antichrist

"and every spirit that does not confess Jesus is not from God. This is the spirit of the antichrist, which you heard was coming and now is in the world already." 1 John 4:3

Anxious Spirit

"As for me, Daniel, my spirit within me was anxious, and the visions of my head alarmed me." Daniel 7:15

Bitter of Spirit

"for they made his spirit bitter, and he spoke rashly with his lips." Psalm 106:33

Spirit of Confusion

"The Lord has mingled within her a spirit of confusion, and they will make Egypt stagger in all its deeds, as a drunken man staggers in his vomit." Isaiah 19:14

Deaf and Dumb Spirit

"And when Jesus saw that a crowd came running together, he rebuked the unclean spirit, saying to it, 'You mute and deaf spirit, I command you, come out of him and never enter him again.'" Mark 9:25

Spirit of the Destroyer

"Thus says the Lord: 'Behold, I will stir up

the spirit of a destroyer against Babylon, against the inhabitants of Leb-kamai,'" Jeremiah 51:1

Spirit of Divination

"As we were going to the place of prayer, we were met by a slave girl who had a spirit of divination and brought her owners much gain by fortune-telling." Acts 16:16

Disabling Spirit

"And behold, there was a woman who had had a disabling spirit for eighteen years. She was bent over and could not fully straighten herself." Luke 13:11

Emptiness of Spirit

"It is better to see what you desire, than to desire what you cannot know. But this, too, is emptiness and a presumption of spirit." Ecclesiastes 6:9

Evil Spirit

"And the man in whom was the evil spirit leaped on them, mastered all of them and overpowered

them, so that they fled out of that house naked and wounded." Acts 19:16

Fornication

"My people have inquired of their stave, and their staff has announced to them. For the spirit of fornication has deceived them, and they have been fornicating before their God." Hosea 4:12

Spirit of the gods

"I have heard of you that the spirit of the gods is in you, and that light and understanding and excellent wisdom are found in you." Daniel 5:14

Grieved in Spirit

"For the Lord has called you like a wife deserted and grieved in spirit, like a wife of youth when she is cast off, says your God." Isaiah 54:6

Grievous Spirit

"And the Lord put a very grievous spirit between Abimelech and the inhabitants of Shechem, who began to detest him," Judges 9:23

Harmful Spirit (Spirit of Torment)

"And Saul's servants said to him, "Behold now, a harmful spirit from God is tormenting you." 1 Samuel 16:15

Spirit of Jealousy

"or when the spirit of jealousy comes over a man and he is jealous of his wife. Then he shall set the woman before the Lord, and the priest shall carry out for her all this law." Numbers 5:30

Lying spirit

"Now therefore behold, the Lord has put a lying spirit in the mouth of these your prophets. The Lord has declared disaster concerning you." 2 Chronicles 18:22

Presumption of Spirit

"It is better to see what you desire, than to desire what you cannot know. But this, too, is emptiness and a presumption of spirit." Ecclesiastes 6:9

Spirit of Princes

"who cuts off the spirit of princes, who is to be feared by the kings of the earth." Psalm 76:12

Spirit of Reluctance

"just as it was written: God has given them a spirit of reluctance: eyes that do not perceive, and ears that do not hear, even until this very day." Romans 11:8

Spirit of Slavery

"For you did not receive the spirit of slavery to fall back into fear, but you have received the Spirit of adoption as sons, by whom we cry, 'Abba! Father!'" Romans 8:15

Terrified Spirit

"My spirit was terrified. I, Daniel, was fearful at these things, and the visions of my head disturbed me." Daniel 7:15

Michelle D. King

Spirit of an Unclean Demon

"And in the synagogue there was a man who had the spirit of an unclean demon, and he cried out with a loud voice,"
Luke 4:33

"For he was saying to him, 'Come out of the man, you unclean spirit!'"
Mark 5:8

Spirit of Whoredom

"Their deeds do not permit them to return to their God. For the spirit of whoredom is within them, and they know not the Lord."
Hosea 5:4

"My people inquire of a piece of wood, and their walking staff gives them oracles. For a spirit of whoredom has led them astray, and they have left their God to play the whore."
Hosea 4:12

From Eric King:

To My Wife:

Life changed for us dramatically in 2018. There were times where I wasn't sure if I would even have a wife and initially, I was very fearful and scared because of what happened. Over the past few years, I have seen that God has used what you had experienced for His good. I have seen, and heard, unexplainable things that can only be explained as miracles. I am glad that you are still my wife and that we are going strong, and that God is still using you in mighty ways.

He sustained not only me but our whole family and has gotten us through some rough seas to where we are now. He was truly with us in that storm of our life and every other storm we have overcome. I am forever grateful to have you in my life as my partner and I pray that God keeps blessing this ministry and it continues to have such a powerful impact on so many people.

I am very proud of you for all of the hard work you are doing for God's kingdom, and I know He is pleased as well.

Your Husband,
Eric

From Michelle D. King:

Thank you, Eric, for never giving up on me and for patiently reminding me of who I truly am. I love you more than words can say.

To my family, thank you for loving me through it all. To my sister, Trisha, God sustained us and raised us up on Eagles wings. We are saved by grace; I am so proud of the woman you have become and your strength in overcoming this too.

To my children, when you read this book, I pray that God will reveal to you why your momma has chosen to give our lives to the purpose of setting the captives free and bringing healing to the broken. Thank you for all the sacrifices you have made for the hurt, the lost, the grieving, the broken, and the traumatized. God is pleased with you.

I love you all.

"Love is patient, love is kind. It does not envy, it does not boast, it is not proud."
1 Corinthians 13:4 NIV